# EQUIPPED AND EMPOWERED

*Preparing Women for Spiritual Battle*

## PAT DOMANGUE

WESTBOW·
PRESS
A DIVISION OF THOMAS NELSON
& ZONDERVAN

WestBow Press books may be ordered through booksellers or by contacting:

WestBow Press
A Division of Thomas Nelson & Zondervan
1663 Liberty Drive
Bloomington, IN 47403
www.westbowpress.com
1 (866) 928-1240

ISBN: 978-1-4908-7288-9 (sc)
ISBN: 978-1-4908-7287-2 (e)

Library of Congress Control Number: 2015903802

Print information available on the last page.

WestBow Press rev. date: 03/20/2015

# CONTENTS

# INTRODUCTION

I am convinced that too many Christian women live defeated lives. Many times we lack biblical knowledge about the spiritual battle and don't recognize Satan's work. Sometimes we do not know how to apply biblical principles to our personal situations. I believe this because I lived defeated for the first five years after Jesus became my Savior when I was thirty years old. My past haunted me. Spiritual chains bound me. My third marriage and my children suffered. Through it all, I continued to read my Bible until I understood the spiritual battle that raged around me and over me.

We are entering into a time of unmatched seduction and deception, and we need to be armed and ready. Evil influences bombard our senses every day through media, culture, images, songs, books, news, etc. Has it been bad before? Yes! In Genesis 6:6, in the days of Noah, God was sorry He had created the human race and wiped the earth clean, leaving only one family to repopulate the world. In Genesis 19:5, the men of Sodom wanted to have sex with the angels God had sent to deliver Lot before He leveled Sodom and Gomorrah.

Thankfully, God has not destroyed us. Does that mean it is not so bad? No, but it reveals the grace we live in and the long-suffering, loving God who wants everyone on earth to know Him, to love Him, to serve Him, and to live for Him.

> The Lord is not slack concerning His promise, as some count
> slackness, but is longsuffering toward us, not willing that any
> should perish but that all should come to repentance.
> 2 Peter 3:9

After years of struggling to experience spiritual well-being and victory, I discovered basic scriptural principles applicable to my real-life circumstances. I began to understand the power I had been given as a child of God and believer in Jesus Christ. God's Word transformed me and taught me how to live in victory over my past and current circumstances and battles. I had spent too much of my adult life being seduced by my own desires, believing lies, and living defeated.

My deep desire is to walk with you through God's Word and help you discover the knowledge and truth needed to equip and empower you in this spiritual battle. Through this study, you will learn the dangers and deceptions we face. You will learn how to combat the enemy and come through victorious in Jesus' name. This is spiritual war—and like it or not, we are in it.

*Equipped and Empowered* offers seven weeks of study. Each week has five days of study designed to take an average of about fifteen minutes. Days 1–4 are a traditional Bible-study style. You will stroll down gold-paved streets on a quest to know God and journey down the enemy's dusty, barren path. You will examine yourself and the lies and deceptions we are so prone to believe. You will study spiritual armor and how to use that armor in your everyday life. On Day 5 of each week, you will read a brief fictional story, with questions from the previous four days of study dedicated to teaching practical biblical application.

Those who complete this seven-week study will be equipped and empowered with the necessary knowledge to live a victorious life in Christ. Let's get started with Week 1 as we establish the nature of the battle.

# WEEK 1

## ESTABLISHING THE NATURE OF THE BATTLE

I spent more than a decade of my adult life deceived by the enemy's lies and seduced by my own desires. Through my twenty-year journey with Christ, I have learned the truth and been set free from a life of bondage to various areas of sinful behavior and addictions. I want to take my experience and walk with you through God's Word, discovering the dangers and deceptions all around us and learning to live a life of victory over our enemy. We are entering into a time of unmatched seduction and deception, and we need to be armed and ready. This is spiritual war, and whether we like it or not, we are in it.

> For our struggle is not against flesh and blood, but against the rulers,
> against the authorities, against the powers of this dark world and
> against the spiritual forces of evil in the heavenly realms.
> Ephesians 6:12 (NIV)

### Day 1
### The Truth Is...

I am so glad you decided to take this adventure with me to study God's Word as it relates to the spiritual battle. Be prepared: the enemy is not going to sit back and let you learn without throwing in hindrances to get you off track. You need to begin this study digging your feet down deep in commitment to learning, knowing that as a result, you will be equipped and empowered to live victoriously over the enemy's work.

Today let's complete the dot, dot, dot of our title, "The Truth is..." Pontius Pilate, the governor who made the call to crucify Jesus, asked Him, "What is truth?" (John 18:38). We are searching out a specific truth for this lesson that will make a major difference in our journey in Christ.

My daughter once loved playing the game Battleship and the card game Battle. There is absolutely no strategy in Battle; however, Battleship does have a method that allows the player to develop a plan of attack. The enemy has a method to his attack. Knowing his method gives us the opportunity to prepare to defend ourselves and to defeat him.

Read John 10:10, and write it on the lines below.

_____

_____

_____

In John 10:10, Jesus said there is one who has a bad plan and one who has a good plan for our lives. Jesus is the one who came to give us abundant life. I have heard the last part of John 10:10 used in church many times, but rarely do I hear the first part of the verse connected to it. I guess it is our human nature to desire to focus on the good aspects of life. The problem is, the bad is still there.

In church, we hear that God has a good plan for us. Jeremiah 29:11 is used probably more than any other passage of Scripture to remind us of His good plan for our lives.

"For I know the plans I have for you," declares the Lord,
"plans to prosper you and not to harm you, plans to give you hope and a future."
Jeremiah 29:11 (NIV)

This is a truth I have held on to throughout my Christian journey. For now, let's set this affirmation aside and focus on what we find difficult—facing the reality of our unseen enemy.

Read 2 Corinthians 2:11 and Ephesians 6:11.

Each verse has a word or words used to portray how the enemy works. Below is a list of various translations; in the blanks, write the words used in your Bible.

|  | 2 Corinthians 2:11 | Ephesians 6:11 |
|---|---|---|
| Your Bible | | |
| NIV | schemes | devil's schemes |
| NLT | evil schemes | all strategies and tricks |
| The Message | sly ways | everything the Devil throws your way |
| KJV | devices | wiles |

The word *devices* in 2 Corinthians 2:11 (KJV) is the Greek word *noema*, meaning an evil purpose. The Greek word for *wiles* in Ephesians 6:11 (KJV) is *methodeia*, meaning cunning arts, deceit, craft, trickery. I hope you see the similarity between the Greek word *methodeia* and the English word *method*. The *Complete Word Study Dictionary* says, "Method, the following or pursuing of an orderly and technical procedure in the handling of a subject." My dear sister, the enemy does have a method to his madness!

Using what you studied in this lesson, complete the dot, dot, dot of today's title.

The truth is...

_____

_____

_____

_____

Here is my conclusion to the truth we are searching for today. The truth is: God has a good plan to prosper us and not harm us, but we also have an enemy who has a methodical, well-thought-out plan for our lives that is evil in all its purposes.

# Day 2
# The Times We Live In

Yesterday we focused our attention on the fact that the enemy has a strategic plan to steal, kill, and destroy in our lives. Today we want to turn our eyes to the world around us. It is not difficult to see the world's condition. The problem for many of us is that we are not taking the time to stop and look. We're busy. We have places to go and people to see and not much time to do it in. But let's take a break from our hectic schedules and busy pace and think through the reality of what is happening in the times in which we live.

Read 2 Timothy 3:1–5, and list all the traits of people living in the last days.

_____

_____

_____

_____

That is not a very pretty list. Do any of these hit home? Could you see yourself or your friends or family members as you read the verses? Step outside of your immediate circle of family and friends, and look around. If you have a TV, smart phone, computer, magazine, newspaper (archaic, I know), or any other source on current events, search it and pick a few examples that connect to the list above.

List what you see happening in the world today, and circle the traits in your list that correspond to those in 2 Timothy 3:1–5.

_____

_____

_____

_____

As I write this, the day's headlines are focused on a mass shooting. Do you see similarities between Timothy's description of the last days and today? Hear the holy alarm sound in 1 Timothy 4:1.

> The Spirit clearly says that in later times some will abandon the faith
> and follow deceiving spirits and things taught by demons.
> 1 Timothy 4:1 (NIV)

Why does it seem that the devil is on a rampage to do as much damage as possible?

Read Revelation 12:12, and write the answer in the space below. Why now?

_____

When I was a little girl, we had a camp on Lake D'Arbonne in Farmerville, Louisiana. I became friends with two sisters a few camps down from ours. They had a fabulous, giant swing made with a board and a scratchy rope perched at the top of a hill overlooking the lake. The swing hung from a limb about fifteen feet above the ground. I would climb onto a retaining wall about ten feet behind the swing, propel myself onto the seat, and soar over the hill below. My stomach would leap to my throat, and I loved it.

One autumn day, just as I passed over the edge of the hill, I caught a glimpse of something long, thin, and black close to the high point of the hill where my feet would touch once my swing lost momentum. On my way back down, I focused on the slithering black line and knew it was my worst nightmare—a snake! I put my vocal chords to the test and probably angered a few fishermen on the lake. My friends' mother burst out the front door while I screamed, "Snake! Snake! Snake!"

She ran in the opposite direction from me and the snake. I continued to scream. Minutes later, I stood frozen with fear as she chopped the snake into pieces with a garden hoe. I was astonished that she'd had the courage to go after that snake with a measly hoe, yet my astonishment increased when she finished dissecting the snake's head from its body, and the headless body continued to slither across the ground.

I once heard a pastor describe the enemy's final rampage. He said Satan is like a mortally wounded snake that still thrashes around for some time after the actual point of death. He might be fighting mad, thrashing around, and doing some damage, but he knows his time is short. The picture of Jesus hanging from a cross and announcing, "It is finished" was his day of doom, and it is still fresh on his mind. Jesus won. The victory is His and ours. Raise your banners high. Hold up your heads, and walk in peace next to Jesus, because He will fight for you (Exodus 14:14)!

## Day 3
## Who Is in Danger of Being Deceived?

So far this week, we have seen that Satan, our enemy, has an evil plan and is in a rage over his ultimate defeat. Today we have a question we must answer. Please read the title question. Turn to the middle of yesterday's lesson, and reread 1 Timothy 4:1.

What clue does 1 Timothy 4:1 give about who is in danger of being deceived?

_____

Turn to Matthew 24:3–5, and fill in the blanks below.

1. Jesus was talking to His _____ about the end of the age.
2. He said, "Take heed that no one deceives _____."

3. He said, "Many will come in my name, saying, 'I am the Christ,' and will deceive

   _____."

Read Matthew 24:24. Whom does Jesus say is in danger of being deceived?

_____

I hope you're getting the picture. We are all in danger of being deceived. We must diligently guard our hearts and minds, because as we've already learned, we have an enemy who has a plan to methodically steal, kill, and destroy our lives. The times in which we live do resemble the last days. And in those last days, there will be many who are deceived, even the elect. But just in case you're thinking, "That won't happen to me—I love the Lord; I'm committed to Him, and I don't think I could be deceived," check out 1 Corinthians 10:12 below. Let the meaning of this warning strike home in your heart and mind.

> Let him who thinks he stands take heed lest he falls.
> 1 Corinthians 10:12

Write out a prayer to God, asking Him to reveal any deception in you and to shield you from the deception of the enemy, today and in the future.

_____

_____

_____

_____

_____

_____

_____

_____

# Day 4

# How Are We Seduced and Deceived?

I hope you've had a good three days in God's Word and learned some important facts about Satan and his work. You now know that Satan has devised an evil plan of stealing and destruction for us because he is in a rage and that none of us are exempt from his deception. For the past three days, we have focused on influences, powers, and people outside of ourselves. Now let His light shine on us.

Read James 1:13–15. What two things does verse 13 say God cannot do?

_____

When are people tempted?

_____

Look at the progression that takes place when we are drawn away by temptation. Finish placing the words below in the proper order according to James 1:13–15.

<u>#1</u> Temptation _____ Death _____ Sin _____ Lust

Lust is enticing. In 2 Peter 2:18, Peter warns about false teachers and how they get their message heard and accepted, "When they speak great swelling words of emptiness, they <u>allure</u> through the lusts of the flesh." The word *allure* in 2 Peter 2:18 and *lust* in James 1:14 are the same original Greek word, with the same meaning.

I love studying the original languages of the Bible, and anyone who has studied with me knows that. A few years ago, I taught a Sunday school class of teen girls; one of them was moving to New Mexico, so we had a going-away party. The girls began teasing me about what I would be like when I got old. They predicted that I would be in a nursing home handing out study guides and trying to explain the Greek and Hebrew meanings of words. The girl moving away quipped, "Mrs. Pat, what is the Hebrew meaning of *Depends*?" Needless to say, we all fell into hysterical fits of laughter!

Well, guess what we are about to do. You got it! We are going to look at the meaning of the Greek word for *lust* and *allure*, which is *deleazo,* meaning to bait or catch by using a bait. *Deleazo* comes from a root word that means craft, deceit, or guile and gives a mental picture of a decoy.

When I was a little girl, my daddy was an avid duck hunter. Avid duck hunters are serious about their decoys! Daddy spent as much time getting his decoys in top-notch condition as he did hunting, because he knew that if he was going to be successful at duck hunting, his decoys would be key to that success. The decoys were placed in the water below his duck blind to entice the ducks by sending this message, "This is a nice place to be. Why don't you join me?"

In the duck blind, my daddy would be sitting with a gun ready to fire and the duck call to his lips. He was good at using the duck call; it sounded as real as the decoys looked. Then, *BAM!* A dead duck. I don't know about you, but I don't want to be a dead duck.

Read 1 Corinthians 10:13. What does God promise will come with the temptation?

_____

Praise His name! Not only does He provide a way out, He provides a way that makes it bearable for us! He is so good!

# Day 5
# Day of Fiction—Apply God's Word

Today you will read about a woman and her personal struggle. You will use the past four Bible lessons to see how God's Word applies to her story. First, read the story. Then answer the questions that follow. Each question will have a reference to the appropriate day's lesson. The purpose of this exercise is to teach us how to relate God's Word to our everyday struggles.

Bursting with joy, Stella could hardly wait to tell her husband, Rod, what God had awakened in her heart. After months and months of searching and praying, she felt aflame inside and knew that a new journey was on the horizon. Once home, Stella found Rod in his recliner, reading the paper. She kissed him and asked about his day. He responded sweetly, "Good—what's for supper?" Stella rattled off the menu and headed for the kitchen. "Oh, baby, I have to tell you about my day."

"Okay, but can you get dinner started and talk? I'm hungry!"

She took a deep breath and replied, "Absolutely."

While cutting up vegetables and preparing the chicken, Stella told Rod of her dreams and passions. He interrupted her. "How much will this cost me, and how much money will it make?"

Deflated, Stella's thoughts raced. What did he just say? Surely he did not just say that my dream will cost him too much. Here I am sharing my heart, and he is bringing up money. Her eyes welled with tears, her throat tightened, and she responded, "I'm only sharing with you what's in my heart. Why can't you just listen?"

Feeling accused, Rod retaliated: "You're talking about taking care of a large piece of farm ground, and you cannot even run your own office without hiring an office manager." Unkind words flew back and forth.

Moments earlier, Stella's heart had been soaring, but now it felt pierced and crushed. Soon she found herself driving away from home, crying uncontrollably. Familiar feelings of rejection crept in. She had taken the bait. Accusations flew through her mind like darts:

You married the wrong man. He will never support your dreams unless they are a cash cow. He doesn't believe in you, just like your dad. He's inconsiderate, selfish, prideful, and hurtful. He's not a team player. His money and hunting are more important than you. He is never romantic. He will never include you in any major decisions. Don't you see? Your Mr. Right is not so right after all.

She continued along winding back roads, crying so hard she could barely see. How could such an amazing day turn into something so heartbreaking? Why did Rod have to be such a jerk? Why couldn't she share her dreams with the man she loved? Why did God tell her to marry him? Why, God? Why? Sure that her friends' husbands were better listeners than hers, she felt alone and angry. Never again would she reveal her true desires to him. She would not divorce him, but she would never again give him the opportunity to pounce on her dreams. He could do his thing, and she would do hers.

Bombarded by negative thoughts, she cried out, "LORD, what are you doing? This hurts! Reveal yourself to me! You uncovered these passions, now what am I to do?" Suddenly, she heard that still small voice from within, "Your fight is not with your husband. Your fight is with the enemy. He wants to kill your dreams, and destroy your future."

Stella pulled over and buried her head in her hands. She realized she had been seduced by the great tempter and had believed his lies. Her tears continued, but she knew God was up to something. Stella recognized that the battle was with the powers of darkness coming against her, not with her husband. Rod hadn't responded the way she had hoped. His words hurt her vulnerable heart, but she knew her Lord had a greater plan. If her King allowed her to hear these awful words, then He would use them for something she could not yet see. Through this pain, God revealed things that needed to be uprooted, addressed, and healed. He allowed her to see deep wounds that colored everything she saw.

How do you see the enemy at work to steal, kill, and destroy in Stella's life? (Day 1)

_____

_____

_____

Compare the list of traits from 2 Timothy 3:1–5 on Day 2 to Stella's story. Can you see any of these in Stella's story? If so, explain.

_____

_____

_____

The story depicts Stella as a Christian, but it also shows that she had taken Satan's bait and believed his lies. How do you think that might have happened? (Day 3)

_____

_____

_____

Try to identify the enemy's decoy or bait in the story. (Day 4)

_____

_____

Did the story or the daily lessons point to any areas in your life where the enemy may be at work? If so, explain.

_____

_____

_____

_____

I am so proud of you for making it through the first week of study. Finish your day by asking God to use this week's lessons to make you more sensitive to the dangers and deceptions that surround you in this world.

# Week 2

## Know the Enemy

I have heard the game of football referred to as a field of battle. Even though I don't have a ball-playing bone in my body, I love sports. My mother was one of the most athletic women I have ever known and taught high school physical education for thirty years. I have teased her that God played a joke on her and sent her a dancer rather than a ball player. However, her love for sports rubbed off on me. While it is hard for me to relate to war, I can relate to football.

Let's think about football as a war. A football game is a three-hour battle on a field. There are two teams opposing one another. One is working to go one direction to the end zone for a score, and the other team is working to stop them. Coaches and players prepare to stop their opponent before they ever step foot on the field by watching films of past games their opponents played. They look for weaknesses, patterns, strategies, who the weak and strong players are, and anything that will give them more information about the team. They thoroughly study their opponent to gain a clear understanding. Therefore, teams are better equipped and prepared once game day arrives.

That is what we are doing—getting to know the enemy and how he works so we can recognize his crafty, evil presence the minute he enters our scene. For you and me, this is not game day; it is real life. We must prepare for the day _when_ we step on the field to face an unseen enemy. You might already be there.

# Day 1
# The Tempter Comes

This week, we will focus our attention on recognizing the enemy and his methods. Recognizing the enemy when he steps on the playing field of our life can make all the difference in how we live life today.

Today's title states a fact, "The Tempter Comes," because he does. If Satan would tempt the flesh and blood Son of God, what would cause him to overlook us? Absolutely nothing! He is aware of our potential as a child of God, and he realizes the power of our testimony (Revelation 12:11).

Look back at this week's introduction, and find the italicized and underlined word in the final paragraph; then circle the same word in James 1:2 below.

> Count it all joy when ye fall into divers temptations.
>
> James 1:2

Temptation is based on the weakness of our flesh, as we learned on Day 4 of last week. At times, God allows us to have a head-on collision with temptation; at other times, it may be much more subtle. Today is about in-your-face temptation. This temptation is intense. It will come, and the tempter will assault you at your weakest points.

Read Luke 4:1–12
How long did Jesus endure temptation (verse 2)? _____
How long had it been since Jesus had eaten (verse 2)? _____
How does verse 2 describe the way Jesus was feeling? _____
Write out Satan's words from Luke 4:3.

_____

Oh my goodness, he plays so dirty! He sticks in the knife and gives it a twist. Whether he is being subtle or all up in your stuff, he is as low down as it gets. There is no mercy with him. When you're down, don't make the mistake of thinking it can't get worse. If the devil has anything to do with it, it will. However, Jesus made it through that first temptation and then went on to endure more temptation before the enemy left him.

Read Luke 4:13. What words tell us that the devil was not finished tempting Jesus?

_____

Read Luke 4:14. How did Jesus return after enduring the temptation?

_____

Enduring temptation and not giving in makes us stronger. The enemy means it for evil, but God allows temptation for a good purpose (Genesis 50:20). Look back at James 1:2. I quoted the KJV above because it uses the word *temptation*. Here, *temptation* is the noun form of the same root word used in verb form, *tempted*, in Luke 4:2. It means an experiment, attempt, trial, or proving. *Divers* means various colors, variegated, of various sorts. Picture in your mind a wooden artist palette with yellow, green, blue, red, brown, and black, and don't forget magenta, lilac, cornflower blue, raw umber, sea-foam green, buttercup, etc. The list can go on and on.

Read James 1:2–4 to discover God's good purpose in our various temptations and trials.

In verse 3, what is being tested? _____

What is good about the testing of our faith? _____

What does perseverance do? _____

I love it! The enemy has plans to trip us up, but God takes his plan and uses it for our completion. He uses the enduring of temptations and trials to ensure that we will not be lacking in anything. You've probably experienced a time when you felt like temptations and trials of every color were being painted on the canvas of your life.

Write a brief description of it.

_____

_____

Blessed is the man who perseveres under trial, because when he has stood the test, he will receive the crown of life that God has promised to those who love Him.
James 1:12 (NIV)

Finish today by asking God to equip and empower you so that James 1:12 can be a reality in your life.

# Day 2
# Roaring Lion

One Sunday afternoon, my husband and I were flipping through TV channels. We stopped on a channel that was reenacting a mountain lion attack in California. Two young women were riding bikes; the soon-to-be victim cycled ahead a short distance in front of her friend. The mountain lion crouched behind the brush on the mountainside and waited for the perfect opportunity to attack (remember Luke 4:13). He lunged at the young woman, sunk his teeth into her neck, and began dragging her down the mountain. Her friend jumped off her bike, grabbed her friend's feet, and screamed for help. Some men heard her screams and rushed to the horrifying scene.

The young woman's face, head, and neck were ripped open and severely damaged. She lived to tell this terrifying story, yet she has undergone extensive surgeries to repair the damage. Though she has some scarring, the surgeons performed what had seemed impossible. They restored her face and wiped away many visible signs of the incident, but for the victim, nothing will ever remove the memory of that day.

She said she felt as though her body would be ripped in half when the lion and her friend clung to opposite ends. One held on with the sole purpose of devouring, and the other hung on to save her life. She said the one thing that stuck in her mind as the lion drug her down the mountain was what incredible, indescribable power the animal had—like nothing she had ever imagined. With this in mind, let's go to God's Word.

Read 1 Peter 5:8.
What two instructions are given to us?
1._____ 2._____
At one point, the Bible gets personal: it says "_____ enemy."
Write down the actions of your enemy.

_____

We cannot miss the personal tone of the message. The enemy is seeking whom he may devour, and he is watching you. I hope you are picturing your enemy hidden and crouching like the mountain lion, focusing on you, watching to see whether you are devourable (my word—not in Webster's).

The enemy is keenly aware of each one of us, and he is looking for our weaknesses. Weakness can come in many forms; today I want to look at one in particular that lines up with a lion's nature. Lions prey on other animals and attack those on the fringes. They look for the one not with the rest. I believe that is a physical picture of a spiritual reality. God designed us for relationship; we need each other, especially in the latter days.

Let us not give up meeting together, as some are in the habit of doing, but let us encourage one another—and all the more as you see the Day approaching.
Hebrews 10:25 (NIV)

According to Hebrews 10:25, what is the reason we need to stay close together?

_____

What if the woman had been biking alone that afternoon? The mountain lion would have devoured her. We need each other for so many reasons; encouragement is huge, but also we need to know we have others surrounding us who will fight for us when the murderer (John 8:44) comes in for the kill!

Before we wrap this up, let's bring yesterday's topic of the tempter together with today's topic of a roaring lion and address living on the outside edge of God's will. When my brother was a little boy, he and my mother were sitting around the dining table, visiting with family. There was a fresh apple pie on the table, and my brother stuck his finger in it and licked the gooey apple filling off his finger. My mother told him he had better not stick his finger back in the pie. So he did what every four-year-old American boy would do. He clasped his hands behind his back, bent over the pie and took a bite out of it without ever engaging his hands!

At times, our walk with the Lord resembles this story. We try to sidestep areas of obedience and live on the fringes, compromising God's best plan for us.

Give some examples of how we can sin and think, Technically, that's not sin.

---

How about a little white lie, gossip, lust, disrespecting our husband…? Most of these are not what people have ranked as "bad" sins (Proverbs 14:12), but to God, sin is sin. Besides, down deep, don't we know better?

Read James 4:14–17.

If someone knows the good she should do and does not do it, that is called _____.

Through a little unchecked sin, we can live on the fringes of God's will and within the sight of our enemy. He is watching closely, hoping to get us away just long enough to devour us or, at least, damage us.

How do we deal with this? Look at the instructions from Peter at the beginning of our lesson today. Remember the instructions from 1 Peter 5:8, and ask God to make you sober and vigilant.

# Day 3

## An Evil Ruler

We studied the enemy as the tempter on Day 1, realizing that if he tempted Jesus, we will also be tempted. On Day 2, we viewed our enemy from the 1 Peter 5:8 perspective, as a roaring lion seeking someone to devour. Today we see that Satan is the god of this world; he is the ruler of demons.

He is not like God, though he wants us to think he is. He is not omnipotent like God but has limited power. He is not omnipresent like God, meaning he can't be everywhere at one time, so he uses demons to do his dirty work. God is omniscient, or all-knowing; the devil and his demons are not. They can't read minds, though they may read your physical actions and body language. With that being said, their attack does begin in our minds. The enemy loves to play mind games, and everyone is fair game (see Week 1, Day 3).

Read 2 Corinthians 4:3–4.
What does the god of this world (Satan) do to the minds of those who are perishing?

_____

What is his purpose in blinding their minds?

_____

I will never forget the day my oldest daughter, Taylor, was lost in the mall. She was six years old at the time, and my younger daughter, Jade, was three. They had just had taken their picture taken with Santa. I bought the Polaroid pictures and handed them to Taylor. (Just in case you are too young to know about Polaroids, they are still images that take a minute or two to develop. They are not instantaneous like taking a photo with a cell phone today.) Taylor was on my left, watching the pictures develop, and Jade was on my right. We headed toward the mall's exit. On the way, I saw a shirt I liked and said, "Let's go in here a minute."

Taylor never heard me. I stepped into the store totally unaware that I was missing one child. Jade dashed in and out of clothes racks, as was her normal practice in stores. I picked up the shirt and looked it over, trying to decide if I really wanted it. Assuming Taylor was in her usual place right by my side, I asked, "Taylor, what do you think about this?" She did not answer. I glanced around and did not see her. I called out a little louder, thinking she was playing hide-and-seek. No Taylor. This time I called Jade, and her dark hair and bright eyes poked out of the dresses hanging in front of me. I asked her where her sister was, and she shrugged her shoulders and said, "I don't know."

A feeling of panic rose up in me. I called Taylor's name louder and louder until I had the attention of everyone in the store. No one had seen her. I walked out into the mall, my mind swirling with fear, and a wave of nausea swept over me. Oh God, please, no! This can't be happening! I stood in the middle of the mall shouting Taylor's name, oblivious to what anyone might think. Then I heard my name over the mall's intercom system, with instructions to report to the mall office. Jade's feet did not touch the floor for the next two minutes, because I snatched her up and ran, with her feet flailing in the air.

Moments later, Taylor and I were holding one another and crying. She told me how afraid she had been for those few minutes that seemed like an eternity to both of us. Taylor had 20/20 vision; she was able to look for help. What if she had been blind?

Explain what you think it would be like if you were lost (in a physical sense) and blind.

_____

_____

Satan is working overtime to close every mind to the truth of God's glorious gospel, because truth sets us free from the enemy's grip (John 8:32). I once watched a program about Herod the Great. He was the king who had all the children in Bethlehem killed when he heard about the Messiah's birth, hoping to kill Jesus

(Matthew 2:16). Herod built a grand fortress on the top of a mountain to protect himself and his kingdom from his enemies. King Herod and his kingdom died. His fortress is now in ruins.

Read John 12:31, 14:30, and 16:11. Fill in the blanks below.

Jesus said, "...the ruler of this world will be _____ _____" (John 12:31).

Jesus said, "...the ruler of this world... has _____ in me" (John 14:30).

Jesus said, "...the ruler of this world is _____" (John 16:11).

The devil has a limited time and a limited title. He is the ruler or the prince of this world, having no hold on Jesus. This world as we know it has an end (Revelation 21:1), and Satan has already been condemned (Revelation 20:10).

Take a minute to write out a prayer for someone who has been blinded by the evil ruler of this world, asking God to remove the scales from his or her eyes and reveal the truth of His gospel to him or her. I challenge you to pray every day for this person until you see his or her eyes opened.

_____

_____

_____

_____

## Day 4

## Accuser, Liar—Cuddly and Deadly

I hope you have learned valuable information regarding the enemy and his methods. Our enemy is a ruler whose power is limited. He is the tempter. He is like a roaring lion seeking someone to devour. This knowledge is not to frighten us but prepare us to recognize him when he appears on the scene of our life.

Today's topic is personal for me because I have believed lies and been deceived more than anyone can know. I have been the victim of the accuser more times than I can calculate (Revelation 12:10). Even writing that sentence, I had the thought that it was my own fault because of my past. That is Satan's mark, always pointing fingers, reminding us of how bad we have been. He brings temptation and puts his crooked finger in our face the moment we make a mistake. Looking back at lies I believed and how I was drawn into those lies blows me away. To remember the degree of my deception is stunning. How does he do it? He lies.

Read John 8:44.

What truth is there in the devil? _____

When the devil speaks a lie, from where are his resources coming? _____

If we lie, where are our resources coming from? _____

Growing up, my girls knew the one thing I hate is a lie. They got off so much easier if they told the truth, but if I caught them in a lie, somebody was going to pay. Lies are never good, even when trying to spare someone's feelings. Lying destroys trust, and trust is essential for any relationship to be healthy.

Tell about a time in your life when you told a lie and it destroyed trust in a relationship.

_____

_____

_____

Has the trust in the relationship been reestablished? _____

Trust can be reestablished, but it takes time. If you are in a relationship that has been damaged by dishonesty, it can be healed. Whether it was you or another who was dishonest, be patient, and don't give up. We were created for relationship, and sometimes those treasured relationships hindered by broken trust can become stronger than before as we work through them and let God bring restoration. There are other times when we make associations with people who are simply not trustworthy.

Do not be deceived: "Evil company corrupts good habits."
1 Corinthians 15:33

Read and reread 1 Corinthians 15:33, and circle the fourth word in the verse.
What is the word you circled? _____
What happens if we keep evil company? _____
Read 2 Corinthians 11:14. Into what does Satan transform himself?

_____

The enemy is crafty. He is good at lying because that is all he has done for the past few thousand years. At times, he comes at us head on; but most of the time, he comes incognito, not looking like a devil at all. I once read an article about white-winged vampire bats that was an amazing parallel to the sly ways the enemy works. The author's life's work was to study the feeding patterns of this particular species of bats. She described the bats as "strikingly appealing," even "cuddly." The picture of them inspired this thought in me: For a bat, it really is cute. She described how they nuzzled her hand and called them "enchanting." Sorry, but I struggled with that one.

She went on to tell how they maintain a close association with their prey, usually a chicken. They feed and sometimes rest in the chickens' feathers for up to eight hours. The chickens become so accustomed to their presence that they will bed down for the night with a bat in their nest or feathers, totally undisturbed by the bat's company. Prior to its bite, the bat licks the wound site until it is numb, so when its razor-sharp teeth sink into the flesh, its prey never knows. Wow! Amazing!

Could it be that we sometimes bed down with the enemy, undisturbed by his presence? Maybe he is numbing our senses to the bite that will drain us of the life God intended for us.

Write a prayer asking God to reveal the enemy in any area of your life to which you have become accustomed to and undisturbed by his presence.

_____

_____

_____

# Day 5
# Day of Fiction—Apply God's Word

Test your learning, and apply God's Word to the fictional story today. Read the story, and answer the questions using the past four lessons. Each question has a reference to the appropriate lesson. We are learning how to relate God's Word to our life struggles.

After another overwhelming and stressful afternoon, Julia pulled herself together, got the kids in the car, and headed to school. As she parked the car, she took a deep breath and reminded herself that her children are a blessing from the Lord. Her husband is a blessing from the Lord. Her home and car are a blessing from the Lord. She has so much to be thankful for. The Lord sees her heart, her fears, and her frustration. He will calm every fear. She can trust her Maker with the heaviness on her heart. He created the universe. Surely He can bring peace in her home.

Julia walked into the gym, where the orientation would begin, and looked around for open seats. As she made her way through the crowd, her eyes fell on someone who had become a little too familiar. The moment Coach Brayden saw Julia, he made his way up the stairs to her. He gave her children high fives. He commented on how pretty she looked, which made her blush. He asked if they needed anything or if they were good with where they were sitting. Something about him brought peace to her heart. As he began to walk down to the gym floor, he turned back and smiled at her. Her heart leapt, and she thought, What is this? I am married with four kids. My husband loves me—or does he?

She pushed the thoughts out and allowed her mind to drift off and think more about the young coach. He always went out of his way to say hello and ask how she was doing. When she had a problem, he listened and encouraged her. When he saw her coming, he waited for her. He opened doors for her. Once, when she was running on the track, he brought her water. He was a little younger than her but so handsome and attentive. She remembered one day when she brought cupcakes for her son's birthday and, as she pulled into the parking lot, she noticed Coach Brayden on the field playing with the kids. He was sweet and controlled—no hollering and screaming and harassing. The kids loved him, and he loved them.

She sensed that he had a crush on her, but she did not feel uncomfortable about that because she was obviously married. She had always been true to her husband and family and intended never to be untrue. They were her priority. Julia would not do anything stupid, for sure.

When things got chaotic around her house, she would simply allow herself to think about what it might be like to be with someone like Coach Brayden, who was focused on her, offering himself to help her, and really in tune with her heart. The thought of his strong arms, gentle smile, and soft touch made her heart skip a beat. But thoughts can't hurt. She had thought about him many times before. No one knew. It was just silly pretending, like reading a good romance novel.

As the orientation ended and she and her children headed home, her anxious feelings began to rise again. What would the house look like when she got home? Would her husband have the younger two kids in bed, or would he still be glued to the TV?

How strong do you think Julia is in relation to temptation? (Day 1)

_____

Is she in danger of falling into temptation? Is there a way of escape? Explain. (Day 1)

_____

_____

What is Julia doing, if anything, to keep her on the fringes? (Day 2)

_____

In what way might the roaring lion devour or do damage to Julia? (Day 2)

_____

_____

Has the enemy blinded or deceived Julia? Please explain your answer. (Day 3)

_____

_____

List any lies in the story. (Day 4)

_____

_____

Relate the story of the vampire bats to Julia's story, and explain. (Day 4)

_____

_____

You did it! Week 2 is complete. I am so proud of you and can't wait to hear how what you learned about the enemy will change your daily decisions and impact your life! Be self-controlled and alert, because you have an enemy; but have no fear, because you have a God who is greater in every way, as we will learn next week.

# WEEK 3

## KNOW THE LORD

Welcome to Week 3. I am so glad to be here with you. You have learned about the spiritual battle and understand that you have a dangerous enemy. This week you will learn about God, who is greater and mightier than our enemy. In an effort to know and understand God's work and plan in our lives, we will focus our attention on vital aspects of His character in relation to the spiritual battle.

> This is eternal life, that they may know You, the only true God,
> and Jesus Christ whom you have sent.
> John 17:3

Before we begin, I must ask, Do you know Him? Have you said yes to Jesus, invited Him into your heart, and given Him the place of Lord in your life?

There is no magic formula to knowing Jesus, but there are important things to understand:

Romans 3:23 – For all have sinned and fall short of the glory of God.

Romans 6:23 – For the wages of sin is death, but the gift of God is eternal life in Christ Jesus our Lord.

John 14:6 – Jesus said to him, "I am the way, the truth, and the life. No one comes to the Father except through Me."

Jesus' call is – "Follow Me" (Matthew 4:19; 8:22; 9:9; 10:38; 16:24; 19:21).

Jesus wants you to walk with Him and give Him the priority position/relationship in your life, allowing Him to be Lord of your life. That decision will affect and change every aspect of your life for good! Here is a simple prayer to help you begin your journey.

Dear Jesus,

I realize that I am a sinner and that I need a Savior. Thank You for offering me the gift of eternal life. I accept that gift. I need you to help me as I begin this journey following You and allowing You to be my Lord and Savior. Please fill me with Your Holy Spirit that I may live equipped and empowered in this life. Help me to choose You and Your ways each and every day.

If you just prayed this prayer, write today's date and a personal commitment to know Him and love Him. If you have done that previously, write the date you did it (as close as you can remember), and write a fresh word of commitment to Him.

Date _____

_____

_____

_____

# Day 1
# Creator

Today we begin a focused look at who God is in relation to the spiritual battle. In Jeremiah 29:13, the Lord declares, "You will seek Me and find Me when you search for me with all your heart." Pray the prayer below.

Precious heavenly Daddy,

I want to know You. Help me to focus on You alone. Please give me a spirit of wisdom and of revelation in the knowledge of You. I pray that the eyes of my heart will be enlightened (Ephesians 1:17–18) as I seek You through Your Word, in Jesus' name. Amen.

Read John 1:1–3 and 14, and fill in the blanks.
"In the beginning was the _____ and the Word was _____ God, and the Word was _____. _____ _____ were made through Him.
"The Word became flesh and dwelt among us" (John 1:14).
What is His name? _____

Jeremiah 32:17 is one of my favorite verses in the Bible. It fits perfectly between these two passages. I challenge you to read Jeremiah 32:17 (below) aloud and with passion. I believe it was written with passion!

Ah, Lord God! Behold, You have made the heavens and the earth
by your great power and outstretched arm. There is nothing too hard for you.
Jeremiah 32:17

Read Colossians 1:13–20.

From what did God rescue us (verse 13)? _____
Who is the image of the invisible God (verse 15)? _____
All things were created by whom and for whom (verses 16–17)? _____
***God made Christ to be the head of the church, the beginning, and the firstborn among the dead so that He might have _____ (verse 18).
List all things He created (verse 16).

_____  _____

_____  _____

_____  _____

_____  _____

_____  _____

King David repeatedly referred to God as the Creator throughout the psalms he wrote. He knew the Lord and knew the power and protection of knowing Him as Creator. The same God who created all things, us included, is the one we call Lord.

Look back at Jeremiah 32:17 and read it again; then read Psalm 124:8.

Finish today by writing out how you can benefit from knowing our Lord as the Creator.

_____

_____

_____

_____

# Day 2
# First in Rank

Yesterday's lesson about God as Creator is reflected in our study today. My goal is not to be repetitive but to give your heart and mind a mega dose of who our God is.

Circle every way you see authority in Ephesians 1:18–23.

I pray also that the eyes of your heart may be enlightened in order that you may know the hope to which he has called you, the riches of his glorious inheritance in the saints, and his incomparably great power for us who believe. That power is like the working of his mighty strength, which he exerted in Christ when he raised him from the dead and seated him at his right hand in the heavenly realms, far above all rule and authority, power and dominion, and every title that can be given, not only in the present age but also in the one to come. And God placed all things under his feet and appointed him to be head over everything for the church, which is his body, the fullness of him who fills everything in every way.
Ephesians 1:18-23

Let's look back at yesterday's lesson.

Look at the list of things in Colossians 1:16 that the Lord created.

Would you say that our enemy falls into any category in this list? _____

Look for the matching fill-in-the-blank sentence, and fill in the blank again.

***God made Christ to be the head of the church, the beginning, and the firstborn among the dead so that He might have _____ (verse 18).

This means that Christ is first in rank. The picture is one of authority. Wikipedia states that "rank is a system of grading seniority and command within armed forces."

Read Matthew 28:18.

What did Jesus say had been given to Him?

_____

Read Luke 7:2–9.

This man understood authority. He amazed Jesus with his great faith. I believe his understanding was a key factor in His great faith. May you and I be given a clear understanding that impacts the faith within us!

Write the centurion's description of how authority works.

_____

_____

_____

Last night my husband and I were watching television. To his delight, I turned on a show about fighter jets on the Discovery Channel. We watched the segment of the program focused on the F22-Raptor. The F22-Raptor was described as the most technologically advanced fighter, with the best computers and best maneuverability. They interviewed a pilot who talked about the jet's incredible performance, making it an unfair fight for its opponent.

I had studied for this lesson the whole day and was blown away by the pilot's words. He said, "The guy who controls the airspace controls the battlefield." Wow!

Our God controls the airspace and the battlefield. When you have taken all you can take, and the enemy has given all he can give, we have a God who is able to do exceedingly and abundantly more than we can ask or imagine (Ephesians 3:20). Let Him have the reins—He already has the reign!

## Day 3

## For You

The first in rank, reigning Creator, who is our God, is for us. I pray this truth gets into the fiber of your being and forever gives you peace in all circumstances. Paul said, "What, then, shall we say in response to this? If God is for us, who can be against us?" (Romans 8:31). His intended answer is, "In Christ, absolutely no one."

Read Deuteronomy 3:22.
What is the instruction? _____
Why did Moses say that? _____

This morning I listened to a preacher's sermon, and he talked about courage as the key to success in any area of life. I thought about the importance of courage when faced with a battle and remembered another sermon I once heard. The pastor said there are 365 places in the Bible where God instructs His people not to be afraid—one for every day of the year. At the same time, His Word tells us that the only one to fear is God himself. Proverbs 1:7 states, "The fear of the Lord is the beginning of wisdom."

Read Exodus 14:14.
What does the Lord do for you? _____
What should you do in response to knowing this?

_____

Have I not commanded you?
Be strong and courageous.
Do not be terrified; do not be discouraged,
for the Lord your God will be with you wherever you go.
Joshua 1:9

We have courage when we have confidence. **We have confidence to have courage when we believe the Lord.** Be honest with yourself, and evaluate your level of confidence in God's Word. Make an X on the line below where you estimate your level of confidence. Zero represents no confidence at all, and 10 represents being fully confident.

| 1 | 2 | 3 | 4 | 5 | 6 | 7 | 8 | 9 | 10 |

Whether you are high or low on the scale right now, I believe that by the end of this Bible study, you will be able to come back to this scale and move your mark closer to the 10. If you already marked 10, then praise His name and ask Him to keep you there!

Today we learned that the Lord our God is for us and fights for us, but let's look at another area in which He is for us. Many times, the enemy tempts us to believe his lies that God's will for us is not good or best. We must establish truth for ourselves so that when he throws this one at us, we can stand firm, knowing, This was for my good.

Read Deuteronomy 10:12–13.
What does God ask of His people (verse 12)?

_____

_____

What did God give for the good of His people (verse 13)?

_____

Read Romans 8:28. What does God work for in all things?

_____

Incredible! In Jeremiah 32:39, God says He will give His people one heart and one way that we may fear Him. He said it is for their good and the good of someone else.

Who is the someone else in Jeremiah 32:39?

_____

Amen!

What a way to speak straight to our hearts. If you are a mom, you know there is nothing we want more for our children than what is good for them. God, the reigning Creator, is for us because He is a perfect parent who always wants what is good for us.

# Day 4
# Always There

Welcome to Day 4. I hope your confidence level in your God is rising with each day of study! There are so many attributes of the Lord, but our objective is to focus on the ones most beneficial during the spiritual battles we face in our daily lives. In the past three days, we've learned that our reigning Creator is first in rank. He is always for us, and He always works all things for our good.

Today we will learn that He is always there. *Always* and *never* are not words I am confident using most of the time, because everyone and everything usually has some variance, but not our God. He is the same yesterday, today, and forever (Hebrews 13:8).

Looking at past personal battles, I realize that my most desperate and panicky moments were the times I did not feel God's presence or think He was there. In the heat of the battle, we must know He is there no matter what.

Our family moved into a new house when my youngest daughter was eight years old. We had a security system for the first time. One night at about midnight, I forgot about the alarm and opened the back door for my cat. The howling alarm shocked my entire nervous system. My heart raced until I was sure my chest would burst open. My daughter's screams penetrated the harshness of the alarm, "Mom! Mom! Mom! Mom! Mom! Mom!" The panic in her voice registered in my maternal depths, and I sprinted up the stairs, skipping every two steps.

My husband had turned off the alarm by the time I saw my hysterical little girl. My heart was pierced as she clung to me. I could feel relief seeping into her body. She looked at me with tears streaming down her face and said, "I didn't know where you were; I didn't know if you were there." I reassured her of her safety, and she spent the rest of that night curled up next to me in our bed.

My presence meant everything to her that night. Her security was in the knowledge of my presence. Our security must be in the knowledge of His presence.

Read Hebrews 13:5–6.

Yesterday we addressed the necessity of courage and confidence in the spiritual battle. Go back to the middle of that lesson; read the bolded sentence and answer the question below.

When can we have confidence to have courage?

_____

Now write what verse 6 tells us we may say with confidence.

_____

Verse 5 tells us the reason we can have confidence to speak these words. What is it?

_____

Look at what else David had to say about God's presence in his life.
Read Psalm 139:7–10. Where did David say he could go to get away from God?

_____

No wonder David said, "His praise shall continually be in my mouth" (Psalm 34:1). Paul also had a propensity to praise God. Look at all he had experienced of God.

Read 2 Timothy 4:17–18.
Write what he had confidence the Lord would do for him.

_____

Finish your day by thanking God for His presence and for greater faith and confidence in all His Word has revealed to you.

_____

_____

_____

_____

# Day 5
## Day of Fiction—Apply God's Word

Glance back over the past four days of Bible lessons; then read the story. Think through how an assurance of the truth taught in the lessons would impact the lives of those in the story. Remember, the purpose of this exercise is to teach us how God's truth can sustain us in our hardest life circumstances.

Tonya's favorite rocking chair was little solace for her broken heart due to her husband Steve's indiscretion and infidelity. They had been married for nineteen years, and another woman was the last thing on her radar. She knew he looked at other women and had never been comfortable with that, but an affair was different. His wandering eyes had hurt her feelings more times than she could count, but he seemed oblivious to how it hurt her. Now she wondered if he simply did not care. She was never really sure, because every time she tried to talk to him about it, he blew her off and said his looking meant nothing because every man looked. That was as far as she could get with that conversation. He hated talking about it, and if she pushed the issue, he would get mad.

She thought back to the times she had looked at his computer history and seen the things he looked at, knowing it wasn't good. At the same time, it wasn't hard-core pornography either. She knew so many women dealing with their husbands' addiction to pornography that this seemed a minor issue. Now she wondered if she should have handled it differently. She had always tried to trust God, knowing that she was not the one who could change her husband; only God could do that. But God had not stopped his looking, and now she was facing a devastated marriage.

Tonya's best friend had never understood how she had handled Steve's looking at other women. Quincie was a fighter and thought Tonya should have fought her husband over the looking issue, but fighting was not her mode of operation. Quincy always got so worked up and upset over how Tonya handled situations with Steve. She didn't want to talk to Quincie right now. Tonya had always joked that if Quincie and Steve had been married, they would have killed each other early in their marriage. Right now, she wished Steve had married someone else, because the pain and rejection she felt was almost more than she could bear.

How would she tell her grown kids that her marriage with their stepfather was over? They had never really accepted him. They saw accepting her marriage to Steve as betraying their deceased father's memory. They were going to be flaming mad and would never forgive him. The best thing she could do for everybody concerned was to keep the truth from them, but could she? What if Steve took the other woman out in public now that he was moving out? She would not be able to keep it from them forever.

Tonya wanted to hate Steve, yet she wanted to help him too. She was concerned about his eternal destiny even though he showed no concern for her when he decided to toss their marriage out the window for a woman thirteen years younger than herself. Tonya wondered if their marriage was beyond repair. Could she ever forgive Steve? Would he continue to see the woman once he moved out, even though he said he wanted their marriage to work out? Would she ever be able to overcome the broken trust in their relationship? The last thing she wanted was to end up like his bitter ex-wife. Steve had fallen into this trap before. He had sacrificed his first marriage for an extramarital affair. That relationship had not lasted after his first marriage ended, but his ex-wife never overcame the poison of her anger.

Tonya knew that the impossible would have to happen if Steve was serious about trying to work it out. She would have to forgive him, trust him, and love him. That was definitely going to take an act of God. It was strange how so many emotions could be mixed up inside her. She longed to run far from Steve and the life they had together. She longed for healing and restoration. She longed for retribution. She wanted to be mad. She wanted to forget. Tonya trusted God's love for her, and she knew her strength would have to come from Him no matter what happened between Steve and her.

Normally, I would not use questions from the introduction to each week, but this week I will. Look back at this week's introduction. What in the story makes you think Tonya had a date in her life when she asked Jesus to be her Lord and Savior? Please explain.

_____

_____

How might Tonya's knowledge of God as the Creator have been life sustaining for her in her present hardship?

_____

_____

What best expresses Christ's authority in this story? (Day 2)

_____

Place an X on the line that you think best represents Tonya's confidence level. (Day 3)

    1    2    3    4    5    6    7    8    9    10

_____

What action could Tonya take that might move her confidence level higher?

_____

Do you think Tonya had confidence that Jesus was always with her? _____
What passages of the Bible from this week of study would you have found the most beneficial to believe if you found yourself in a hardship similar to Tonya's?

_____

# WEEK 4

## Know Who You Are

In his book *The 15 Invaluable Laws of Growth*, John Maxwell writes, "You must know yourself to grow yourself." Knowing who you are is a vital element of being equipped and empowered in the spiritual battle. What are your strengths? Where are you weak? You must know yourself to be able to live victoriously.

This week we will take an assessment of our personal strengths and weaknesses. Sometimes this can be the hardest assessment of all. We can easily see other people's strengths and weaknesses, but our own are harder to identify. However, this valuable understanding can prepare us for temptation, deceptions, or potential dangers the enemy throws our way.

## Day 1
## In the Flesh

How many times have I said, "That goes against my nature" or "That is just the way God made me"? Everyone has said something similar at some point in his or her life. I once attended a conference that focused on personality types as a tool to help speakers and teachers improve in their weak spots and positively use their strengths in ministering to others. I loved learning about personality types. Once I discovered my own, I saw my strengths and weaknesses. Scripture tells us about some natural tendencies of mankind. Warning! You might not like this.

Read Genesis 6:5. Write what God saw in people's thoughts and in their hearts.

_____

Genesis 6:5 happened before God flooded the earth and destroyed all mankind, excluding Noah's family. What did God say about the heart of humanity after the flood in Genesis 8:21?

_____

We have a natural inclination to evil in our hearts, even from our childhood. Let's take a peek at Paul's understanding of his own natural inclination.

Romans 7:5 and18.
What is at work in us when we are in the flesh (verse 5)? _____
What good does Paul say is in our flesh (verse 18)? _____
What does he say is present (verse 18)? _____
What could Paul not find in the flesh (verse 18)? _____
Read Romans 8:8. What is impossible in the flesh? _____

I am not looking at who we are in the flesh to see what a despicable mess we are so that we can go dig a hole somewhere and bury our wretched selves in it. Just as the leaders of the personality conference understood the value of recognizing weaknesses in our personalities, we can see the same principle here. If we understand who we are in the flesh, the knowledge of the weakness can make us stronger.

Read Romans 7:19–25.

Can you relate to Paul's struggle? Tell about a time when you knew the right thing to do, wanted to do the right thing, but could not for the life of you do it.

_____

_____

Let's end on Paul's final understanding when he asks this question: "Who will rescue me from this body of death" (Romans 7:24)? His immediate response to his own question is one of rejoicing and thankfulness because he has the answer (Romans 7:25). Circle the answer to Paul's question from Paul's statement in Romans 8:2 (below).

Through Christ Jesus the law of the Spirit of life set me from the law of sin and death.

Romans 8:2

# Day 2

# In the Spirit

Today's lesson comes on the heels of yesterday's hard lesson addressing our weaknesses in the flesh. In Christ we are called to walk no longer in the flesh but in the Spirit (Romans 8:9); however, our minds need transforming (Romans 12:2) to believe that and live it out. We need to understand living in the Spirit and the benefit of the Spirit-led life. The only way our minds will be able to process, understand, and rearrange our old thinking is if the Holy Spirit does it.

Prayer is essential. Ask God to give to you a spirit of wisdom and revelation in the knowledge of Him, that the eyes of your understanding be enlightened. Use Ephesians 1:17–18 as your prayer. It is powerful. Then let's dig in!

Read Romans 8:9. How do we know that we are in the Spirit and not in the flesh?

_____

Look back at the end of yesterday's lesson and see how Paul answered the question, "Who will rescue me from this body of death?"
Write Paul's question as if asking yourself.

_____

Write Paul's answer, which is also our answer.

_____

Knowing our strengths is as important as knowing our weaknesses. Remember that it is through Christ Jesus that we overcome the weakness of our flesh.

Read Psalm 18:1–2, 32, and 39.
Who is our strength (verses 1–2)? _____
How is He our strength (verses 32 and 39)? _____
Why does He arm us with strength (verse 39)? _____

Jesus arms us with strength by giving us His Spirit. We are ready for battle because He is ready for battle and lives in every believer's heart. Textbooks are usually not exciting, but they do have greater potential to be exciting if the textbook is about the Lord. While reading *A Survey of the Old Testament* for my seminary class, I came across something that was perfect for this portion of our study. I knew God was teaching me to teach you, and that was not a coincidence. That's exciting!

The textbook explained that God is seen in Joshua 10:14 "as engaging in combat on behalf of the Israelites as a divine warrior" and that "Moses addressed Yahweh (the personal name for God) as one going forth in battle (Numbers 10:35)." How incredible our God is! He not only arms us with strength, He arms us with himself, the divine warrior who goes forth in battle.

Read Acts 1:8. What is Jesus' promise when the Holy Spirit comes upon His disciples?

_____

Read 2 Timothy 1:7. What kind of Spirit did God give us?

_____

> Now to Him who is able to do exceedingly abundantly above all that
> we ask or think, according to the power that works in us.
> Ephesians 3:20 (NKJV)

According to Ephesians 3:20, where is God's power at work? _____

Finish the lesson with Ephesians 1:19–22.

Explain the potential and limitations of His power.

_____

_____

# Day 3

# His Child

So far this week, we have studied who we are in the flesh and who we are in the Spirit. When it comes to spiritual battle, the flesh is our weakness and the Spirit is our strength. I loved yesterday's lesson and want to make one connection back to it before we move on to today's lesson. Romans 8:15 and John 1:12 explain another facet of the Spirit we received. Read the scripture passages and answer the questions below.

> To all who received him, to those who believed in His name,
> He gave the right to become children of God.
> John 1:12 (NIV)

> For you did not receive a spirit that makes you a slave again to fear, but
> you received the Spirit of sonship. And by him we cry, "Abba, Father."
> Romans 8:15 (NIV)

Who has the right to become children of God?

_____

When Christ came to live in us, what Spirit did we receive?

_____

What name do we cry out? _____

Don't let the terminology of *sonship* trip you up. You and I, as daughters are included. Romans 8:15 in the New Living Translation says, "You should behave like God's very own children, adopted into his family. We belong to God's family. We are His children.

A few years ago, our family was invited to our first Passover celebration at our Jewish friend's house. All who attended, other than my family, were from Israel. A little boy grabbed my attention the minute he stepped in the room. He was adorable, with dark skin, black silky curls, and an Israeli accent. I thought, Jesus was probably a lot like him when He was a little boy.

At one point during the evening, the little boy jumped into his father's lap, wrapped his little arms around his neck, and called him Abba. Tears stung my eyes at the love I saw between this Abba and his son. You may have heard the saying, "Anyone can be a father, but it takes someone special to be a daddy." *Abba* to the Jew is like saying "Daddy" to me and you.

Read 1 John 3:1. What has the Father lavished on us? _____
We are now called _____.

I love being His child. Having my own children has taught me the value of realizing that I am a child of the Most High God. We talked about how God fights for us in last week's lesson, and today we understand why. I love and adore my three girls, even when they make me crazy. No one can mess with them without stirring Mom's wrath.

When my oldest daughter, Taylor was in first grade and I was picking her up from school one day, she climbed in the backseat of the car and burst into tears. She had been asked by the teacher to write something on the board. Another little girl was angry that she had not been chosen and hit Taylor on the center of her back with a chalk-covered eraser. It left a mark on her clothes, and she was humiliated and devastated.

I was furious at this first grader for hurting my child's feelings and embarrassing her. I wanted to march into that school and turn that child over my knee and make her be nice to Taylor.

This may be a silly story of my wanting to take revenge on a first grader for hurting my six-year-old daughter's feelings, but I really felt that way. The reality is, earthly parents will fight for their children, and nothing makes them more angry than someone hurting them. There is a love in the heart of parents for their children that is impossible to explain; it simply must be experienced. Being a parent affects the heart more than any other experience other than salvation.

I once heard a Bible teacher say, "If God had a refrigerator, He would have your picture on it." Maybe your picture is not posted on some holy refrigerator, but you do have the attention of your heavenly Father. Let's look at Moses' song of worship to God in Deuteronomy 32.

Read Deuteronomy 32:10–11. How does Moses say in verse 10 that God kept him?

_____

What parental picture does he give in verse 11 of God doing this?

_____

The apple of His eye means we are the center of His attention. Raised as an only child because I was a late-in-life surprise, I was accustomed to having all the attention, which went along with my mostly sanguine personality. I loved putting on shows and displaying my wide range of talents for my parents. One of my favorites was a fashion show in which I was the star model and my clothes and accessories came from their closet. Mom's gowns gaped open and hung in heaps at my feet, and I had to pin Dad's boxers to his t-shirts to keep from losing them during the show. I was a sight, but I was the apple of their eye because they loved me and paid close attention to even the goofy things I did. God's focus is on His children, and He tenderly cares for them as the eagle does her young.

This is what the Lord Almighty says:

> "After he has honored me and has sent me against the nations that have plundered you—for whoever touches you touches the apple of his eye..."
> Zechariah 2:8 (NIV)

Take time to summarize what you learned about your heavenly Father today in a prayer of thanksgiving for the treasures of His perfect parental love.

_____

_____

_____

_____

_____

# Day 4
# More Than Conquerors

Do you realize you are over the halfway hump? Good job! Galatians 6:9 says, "Let us not grow weary while doing good, for in due season we shall reap if we do not lose heart." That is His word of encouragement for you to keep up the good work!

So far, you should have identified your flesh as your weakness and the Spirit in you as your strength in the spiritual battle. You are one of God's loved children, and Scripture makes that clear when we look at ourselves through His eyes. In the flesh, we were loved. Our sin nature is what motivated God to perform the greatest act of love known to man, sending and sacrificing His only Son (John 3:16). In the Spirit, we are a reflection of His love that refused to leave us alone in the battle. Being adopted as His children intensifies the reality of His love. Today's lesson is about the win, the victory in the battle.

Read Romans 8:31–39. What is the overriding theme of this passage?

_____

Fill in the blanks using verse 37: "We are _____ than _____
through Him who _____ us."
Paul believed there was no power that could separate us from the love of Christ.
What verb did he use in verse 38 to describe his belief in the powerful love of Christ?

_____

Are you convinced? I am convinced that we must be convinced of His love for us. Being convinced of God's love for us must be a dominant factor to live the conqueror's life. There is an unwaveringness about the one who is convinced. I can say, "I believe," or I can say, "I am convinced." Which statement declares the strongest stance?

This leads us to faith. "Now faith is the substance of things hoped for the evidence of things not seen" (Hebrews 11:1). Faith is being convinced that something is real even when there is nothing tangible to hold on to. Most of us tend to waver at that point. If we have believed for a long time for something, and God allows nothing tangible to come our way, it gets really hard to stay convinced. However, if we keep on believing, we reap stronger faith.

My daughter Avery hates fruit. I remember when she was four years old and we were in the produce aisle of the grocery store, she held her nose as we passed by the fruit, saying, "Ooooh yuck, fruit." Then, coming to the vegetables she said, "Oh yum, broccoli. Mom, can we have broccoli?" Eyeing everything green, she said, "Asparagus! Mom, can we have asparagus too?" Unaware that she had the attention of everyone in the produce section, she spied her favorite, mushrooms. "Mom, please let's get mushrooms." That was all it took to draw comments out of the amazed people nearby. They had never seen anything like it, and neither had I.

The funny thing is, we can't figure out at what point Avery became convinced that fruit tasted bad and vegetables tasted good. She ate fruit as a toddler, but somewhere along the way, she made up her mind that she did not like it anymore. She has not had any fruit in years (not because I have not tried to persuade her) because she is convinced she does not like it. There is no tangible reason I can see that caused her to hate fruit; she just does. This is the kind of convinced we need to be about Christ's love for us—unwavering even when there is nothing we can touch or see on which to base our beliefs.

I think it is rather hilarious that the Lord has me writing about this, because right now, this is my greatest struggle. I have believed God for a long time for one particular thing, and He has not allowed it. In fact, He has not allowed anything that would help convince me. However, I know He has not forgotten me or my desire or His promise.

The more time passes by without an affirmative answer from God, the harder it is to stay convinced. However, that is when we need to dig deeper into the truth of His Word and root ourselves in belief—to stay convinced of His love, His promise, and His faithfulness. We can know He is doing a good work in us. God increases our faith during these hard times and builds our character.

Commit your way to the Lord, trust also in Him, and He shall bring it to pass.
Psalm 37:5 (NKJV)

Read 1 John 5:1–5.
Who is born of God (verse 1)?

_____

Whatever is born of God does what (verse 4)?

_____

What is the victory we have that overcomes the world (verse 4)?

_____

Thanks be to God! He gives us the victory through our Lord Jesus Christ.
1 Corinthians 15:57 (NIV)

# Day 5
# Day of Fiction—Apply God's Word

I hope these stories are helping you connect God's Word to your own everyday life. Sometimes it is easier to see God and the enemy at work in someone else's life than our own. Realizing the Lord's work is vital to living a victorious life. Today's story may be more radical than your own, or you may feel your story is worse; but we all struggle. Glance back at this week's lesson to remember the key Bible-study points. Then read today's story and answer the following questions.

The snare of the enemy's entrapment began innocently enough, one lie at a time. Cecelia was raised in a Christian home. The church they attended emphasized ritualistic worship and works to earn God's love. This first veil of deception was placed over her eyes and heart at a very early age.

In her family, perfection wasn't an option; it was expected. Her father had difficulty expressing affection for his little girl, and her mom leaned on her emotionally to compensate for the dysfunctional marriage. Satan used family relationships to convince Cecelia that if she were good enough, her father would love her more and her parents' marriage would be perfect. Another veil of deception fell over her eyes and heart.

Cecelia strived to fit in high school but carried so much shame over her inability to be perfect that it kept her from allowing anyone to get too close. If only someone had told her about God's unconditional love, maybe she wouldn't have tried to conform to the image of others' expectations. She longed to belong. She dreamed of having someone in her life who would love her for who she was, but Cecelia struggled with loving herself. It became easier for the enemy to deceive her. She was unaware the condemning thoughts she struggled with were placed there by the enemy himself. In desperate attempts to gain attention and acceptance, she looked for love in places that furthered the enemy's purpose. Another veil of deception was placed over her eyes and heart.

Desperate for love, Cecelia found herself in an abusive relationship. She believed she deserved the physical and emotional abuse she endured. Satan had spent years distorting the truth and filling her mind with lies. She wondered if life was worth living. The evil one whispered barbs of criticism that echoed in her mind like a broken record. You don't deserve to be loved. No one will ever love you. God doesn't care about you. You have messed up too many times now, and God will never forgive you.

The shroud of shame became her armor for many years as she continued to be fooled by the guile of Satan. Now, married with a young child, she began to have flashbacks of her parents' dysfunctional relationship that played out in her own marriage. The pain was too much!

Satan's next trap was the attention of her boss. His affirmation and flattery seemed like answers to her prayers. Veils of lies continued to drop over her eyes and heart. As quickly as the affair began, Cecelia realized her horrible mistake. She cried out to God to help her. She felt as though she were hanging from a cliff, about to descend to a place from which she could not return.

God heard her cries and began to help her remove the veils until she could see the web of deceit the enemy had created. The Lord covered her and lifted her out of the deep dark pit. He was gentle and kind. He lovingly guided her back to himself as she submitted more and more to His will. He was faithful to His Word and never left her side as she dealt with the consequences of her choices.

Twenty years later, Cecelia looked back and pondered the things God had taught her since she met Him at her lowest point. She would never wish that anyone would have to travel that same rocky path she traveled, but neither would she trade the pain she had endured. It was through those experiences that she met an awesome God who had loved her all along.

In what ways can you relate to Cecelia's story and struggles?

_____

_____

In what way did Cecelia show that she was ruled by her flesh or sin nature? (Day 1)

_____

_____

Was there evidence that she was walking or had ever walked in the Spirit? (Day 2)

_____

How could the Holy Spirit's living in her have made a difference in the beginning of her story? (Day 2)

_____

What might have been her greatest struggle in knowing God as a loving Father? (Day 3)

_____

_____

Did she ever become more than a conqueror? _____

Do you see any veils of lies in your own life that are similar to Cecelia's? Any bad decisions you need to turn over to God and allow Him to begin cleansing and healing you? Is there any area of life in which you need victory? Christ Jesus is your answer. Take some time to pray and lay your burdens bare before the one who loves you with perfect love.

_____

_____

_____

_____

_____

# WEEK 5

## LIES WE BELIEVE

We are predisposed to be lie believers. We have been since humankind stepped on the scene in Genesis. There are many other lies than what we will address this week, but I've collected some of the most common lies we accept and act on. I have taken Satan's bait on every one of these lies, so the only reason I am able to identify them is because of personal experience. I have also seen other women taking the bait where these lies are concerned. I pray this week will be revealing and freeing for you!

### Day 1
### God Is Holding Out, and You Are Missing Out

Today we begin where we first see the enemy of our souls in the Bible. I pray you recognize the significance of the first glimpse into his methods. He works to deceive and he always has. Let's get started identifying our spiritual enemy's work and deception.

Read Genesis 3:1–6.
There are three firsts in Genesis 3:1–6:

1. This is the first time we see the enemy in Scripture.
2. This is the first time a lie is presented to humankind.
3. This is the first time a woman believed a lie.

What description does Genesis 3:1 give of the enemy? Please fill in the blank.

"The serpent was more _____ than any of the wild animals."

However your Bible translated the word you filled in the blank above, the original Hebrew word means "crafty." The *American Heritage College Dictionary*, 4th Edition, defines *crafty* as: "skilled in or marked by underhandedness, deviousness, or deception." That gives me the idea that he knew exactly what he was doing and went after the woman with intent.

In Week 2, we focused on knowing the enemy. Take a minute to remember and write down as many descriptions as you can about the enemy. If you need to sneak a peak, go ahead.

_____

_____

Let's shift gears and talk about the word *obey*.

What does the word *obey* bring to your mind? How does it make you feel?

_____

_____

*Obey* is one of those words that can get under my skin. Naturally speaking, it is not a word that sets well with most of us. When it comes to obeying God, I believe our greatest hang-up stems from the very first lie presented to humankind in Genesis 3:1. Maybe after these thousands of years, the enemy has gotten better at making us believe it. But one thing that is consistent about our decision not to obey God is our deep-seated belief that God is holding out, and we are missing out. Let's take the first lie and break it down.

Glance back at Genesis 3:1–6.

The enemy said, "Has God indeed said..." (NKJV) or, as the NIV renders it, "Did God really say...."

Whom is the enemy calling into question? _____

He begins with an attack on God's character. If he can shake our belief and cause us to doubt God, His integrity, and His motive, the deceiver knows he may have half a leg to stand on in his deception. I want you to see the next way he caused Eve to question God. Fill in the rest of the enemy's question.

"Has God indeed said, You _____ _____ eat of _____ _____ of the garden."

Read Genesis 2:16–17.
Please write out the words God said in verse 16 only.

_____

Compare and list any differences between what God had "indeed said" and what the enemy implied that God had said.

_____

_____

    Please do not miss the underhandedness of the enemy's message. When I read Genesis 2, I could see God standing next to Adam, spreading his arms out wide to present this huge expanse of land filled with lush green trees and plants and filled with ripe fruits. In my terminology, God was saying, "Adam, look all around—everywhere you see, everything you see is yours to enjoy. There is only one tree in the midst of all this that will not be good for you, so don't eat its fruit."

    When I read Genesis 3:1, I could see the enemy taking the woman straight to that one tree, pointing to it, and saying, "God is holding out on you. He said you can't have everything out here. Look right here. God is holding out on you."

    Can you see the difference in the focus? Everything the enemy does with Eve in the next few verses builds on that lie until she bites into the most costly fruit ever.

Let's end today's lesson by focusing on the truth God wanted Adam to see when He presented that lush garden to him in Genesis 2.

Blessed be the Lord, who daily loads us with benefits, the God of our salvation!
Psalm 68:19

Dear sister in Christ, God is not holding out on you!

# Day 2

# What Is Right in Front of You Is Better Than What Is to Come

Yesterday's lesson was a sister to today's. In Day 1, we learned one lie that we tend to believe: that God is holding out on us. Look back at the last sentence from yesterday's lesson, and read it out loud and to yourself. Then you are ready for today's lesson.

Read Genesis 25:27–34.
In your own words, what was Esau saying in verse 30?

_____

Esau may be the male version of a drama queen. He took the statement, "I'm starving to death" to a whole new level. In his tired and hungry state, he sold his birthright for just a bowl of beans.

I have a pastor friend from seminary who once told me about a date he had with a woman thirty years ago. It was etched in his mind forever. Some date! He said the woman was beautiful, and he could not wait to take her out. He really wanted to impress her, so he took her to the nicest restaurant with the best steaks. He was sure that she would be impressed with him. But when it came time to order dinner, she ordered a bowl of red beans and rice. He was floored. He could not believe that she had settled for just a bowl of beans when she could have had filet mignon. He never took her out on a date again.

Sometimes I think we do the same thing as Esau and this woman. We settle for a bowl of beans when steak is on the menu and somebody else is buying.

Tell about a time when you settled for less than the best and later realized your mistake.

_____

_____

That was a somewhat presumptuous request, but other than those who are very young, with few life experiences, most of us can look back on our lives and recall settling for something only to realize later that we could have done better. We need to self-evaluate to ensure that we are not selling out for what is temporary rather than holding out for what is lasting.

What about now—are you selling out in some area of your life right now? If so, why? I believe it is because we believe a lie. Esau believed a lie—he believed that what was right in front of him was better that what was to come. That's why he didn't hold out but sold out.

Take a moment to evaluate your life. Could you be selling out in some area? If so, describe how.

_____

_____

I have a sweet, young, single friend who told me that God had spoken to her, using this same passage of Scripture to tell her that the man she was interested in was not "the one." A relationship with this man would be selling out for a bowl of beans rather than holding out for her filet mignon. She had to make a decision, and her decision did not come easy; but she made it because she did not want to miss out on what Jesus had for her. She did not believe the lie but clung to the truth of God's Word and trusted in her God, knowing that He is trustworthy.

On the other hand, I have seen similar scenarios play out very differently. Sometimes people want something so badly that they ignore God. Being in ministry, I have had my share of opportunities to minister to women who are in messes because they chose not to heed God's warnings. How many Christian women have ignored 2 Corinthians 6:14, "Do not be unequally yoked," and married an unbeliever? How many knew there was a drinking problem before they said "I do" and lived a nightmare married to an abusive alcoholic? How many women saw signs of unfaithfulness, maybe even married the man with whom they'd had an affair, then lived in a marriage devoid of trust?

God does not give us parameters because He's trying to hold out on us; He gives us parameters to protect us.

At the beginning of today's lesson, I described Esau as a male drama queen. What about his brother? I want to point out his role in all of this, because it will matter to you and me as well. Let's describe Jacob as an opportunist. He saw an opportunity to further his own cause, to gain something for himself no matter how he got it or who got hurt in the process. There will always be opportunists lurking around, waiting for an open door. And they will not be concerned about how they get what they want or whom it hurts.

In the personal stories you shared today, can you see any opportunists on the scene? If so, describe how you see their role in the situation.

---

## Day 3

## You Are Not Enough, and Man Is Enough

Well, dear sister, do you understand that God is not holding out on you and that sometimes the enemy dangles something before our eyes to get us to settle for less than God's best for us? He is quite talented at finding opportune times, when we are weak and worn down, to present his lie.

Today we take a journey through one woman's story to see two interwoven lies. Many times these lies are woven into our own stories.

Read John 4:6–18.

Verse 9 lists two problems that the woman identified as reasons she was puzzled about Jesus' talking to her. Can you identify them?

1. She is a _____. 2. She is a _____.

If you filled in the blanks with *woman* and *Samaritan*, you were right. Being a Samaritan woman in her day and culture was a double whammy. Women in her day were considered greatly inferior to men, so much so that a Middle Eastern man would not even speak to his own wife, mother, or daughter in public. That would be a pretty significant blow to a little girl's self-esteem.

There are loads of statistics that show how devastating it is to a young girl if her father is not actively engaged in her life. The enemy uses this to distort the truth and send the message, "You are not enough." The woman of John 4 was born into a culture that looked down on women and imposed the message, "You are not enough." I believe the enemy sets out to chisel away at our self-esteem at a very early age. This message has his fingerprints all over it.

Was your father actively engaged in your life? _____
How did that affect your life?

_____

_____

Let's look at the woman's second problem: she was considered unclean from birth because she was a Samaritan. The Jews of that day hated the Samaritans because they were a racially mixed people. They were considered unclean—so much so that strict Jews would take the long way around on a journey just to avoid Samaria. They would go around on the east side of Samaria, which involved crossing the Jordan River. An unclean person was to be avoided at all costs by any serious Jew. Many believed that even a Samarian's gaze or breath would make a Jew unclean.

> *Zondervan's Illustrated Bible Backgrounds Commentary* explains: "Samaritans were thought to convey uncleanness by what they lay, sat, or rode on. Samaritan women, like Gentiles, were considered to be in a continual state of ritual uncleaness: 'The daughters of the Samaritans are [deemed unclean as] menstruants from their cradle.'"

Feeling and believing that you are unclean has a powerful affect. When I was thirteen, a fifteen-year-old boy forced himself on me. I knew I was unclean from that moment on. For the next seventeen years, I acted out of that unclean state. Every decision I made was filtered through the effects of that night and the unclean state I knew myself to be in. This was not my fault, and it was not the woman's fault that she was born a Samaritan in a day when others looked down on females and on her race.

Many times, the hideous seeds of the lies the enemy plants begin with something that is totally beyond our control, and we buy into the lie, "You are not enough." The truth is, you are enough. The King greatly desires your beauty (Psalm 45:10), and you are fearfully and wonderfully made, because His works are marvelous (Psalm 139:14).

Look back at John 4:18; what did Jesus identify as the woman's problem?

---

Can we just say, too many men! This woman believed that a man could satisfy her. She sought men to give her fulfillment. My husband is a precious, godly man who adores me, and I adore him, but he comes up short. Some of you have believed another person would be able to fill the void, heal the pain, or at least numb it. But human love is never enough. The Lord built us in such a way that no one and nothing could ever fill the space that He designed for himself alone to fill. I tried to fill my life with men, other religions, alcohol, you name it—I tried almost everything. I found that I was never satisfied, and these other things always cost me too high a price.

Can you point out anything or anyone in your life that you have used to find satisfaction and fulfillment?

_____

_____

What was special about Jesus' offer to the Samaritan woman in John 4:14?

_____

Read Psalm 107:8–9.

Who is the one who satisfies? _____

What does He fill us with? _____

Here is the truth. God's love and goodness are always enough, and they last an eternity!

# Day 4

# Too Much for God

The last lie we are going to look at is the one the enemy lays on top of all the rest. We have not drained all the enemy's resources—he still has loads of other lies—but the lies we have dealt with in this study are too easily accepted by females. I bought into today's lie hook, line, and sinker. (If you have no clue, that is a fishing term.)

Read John 4:6–18.

Use today's title to help fill in the blanks and identify another lie.

You are _____ big of a _____, even _____ _____.

Look back at yesterday's lesson, and write down every problem that might have led the Samaritan woman take the enemy's bait and believe today's lie.

_____

_____

This woman had issues for sure! She was the epitome of the insecure woman with super low self-esteem. She went from man to man in search of someone who would value her and give her self-worth. With each failure, I am sure it wedged her issues deeper into how she identified herself—as an impossible mess.

But the truth is... (read Jeremiah 32:17).
What was God able to accomplish by His great power?

_____

Does His accomplishment seem like a bigger thing than our messes? _____
Write the last sentence from Jeremiah 32:17.

_____

One day, I was driving my youngest daughter to school and praying blessings over her. I had a CD of worship music playing, and in the middle of the song, the church's pastor began praying. He said, "Oh, God, I thank You that that there is nothing to hard for You."

It hit me like I had never heard it before.

I said, "Avery, did you hear that?"

"What, Mama?"

"That there is nothing too hard for our God. No matter what you have to face today, it is not too much or too big for God. Nothing, nothing, nothing."

"Mama," she said, "you are so weird!"

I laughed. "I know, Avery, but I really believe what I am saying."

"I know," she said.

No matter what lies you have believed, no matter how much you have messed up.... You see, I am on my third marriage. Do I like admitting that? Absolutely not. But it is the truth, and I want God to use my mess-ups to help others.

I came to Christ six months after I married my third husband. I was an alcoholic and had a really ugly past. I was married at age sixteen, then at nineteen, then at thirty. I had spent most of my adult life in deep fascination with the occult. When I came to Jesus, I was a mess. If I was not too big of a mess for God, neither are you, and neither is anyone else you know. God is huge!

Jesus came to offer us the gift of life. That life is not just for eternity but for the here and now. In John 4, He tells the woman about the gift He had for her if she would only ask for and receive it. He called the gift "living water" and said that it would spring up into a fountain of everlasting life. In John 10:10, Jesus said, "The thief does not come except to steal, to kill, and to destroy, but I have come that you may have life and life more abundantly."

Take some time to dig down deep and search your soul for what it is in your life that you believed was an impossible situation, your "too much for God." Ask God to forgive your unbelief and to help you believe that He can and He will. Write out your impossible situation and your commitment to entrust it to God. Tell Him you are going to keep believing until He changes the situation.

---

# Day 5

# A Day of Fiction—Apply God's Word

Today's story is about a young mom overwhelmed with busyness and the demands of her everyday life. Even if you aren't a mom, most of us can identify with the sense of overwhelming demands. While your story may look different, focus on the heart of the message to help you identify personal struggles in your life.

Jackie quickly unloaded groceries from her car. She had to be back at the school in one hour. Her husband had agreed to watch the smallest two children while she and the oldest two went to the meeting. She told the kids to start their homework and threw a load of clothes in the drier. She began preparing Taco Delight. While stirring the meat, she heard her oldest son and youngest daughter arguing. She yelled at them to stop fighting and do their homework, but nothing changed.

Her cell phone rang. It was her mother. Ever since her dad's major accident two years earlier, Jackie feared that something tragic would happen to him. Time was pressing, but she must answer. Her mom began complaining about how long it had taken her to answer the phone. Jackie exhaled. Her dad had fallen in the parking lot earlier that day but was okay. Jackie let out a sigh of relief. Her mom insisted that Jackie needed make the three-hour trip to visit her father at least once every two weeks because of his deteriorating health, adding, "And you never know..."

Jackie knew that what her mom said was true, but how in the world could she do it all? Four children, their activities, housekeeping, cooking, the Bible-study group she led, the lonely friend she mentored weekly, bookkeeping for her husband's business, and of course, the daily exercise routine—that was her only time alone. She hung up the phone with a heavy heart.

Her husband, Brad, walked in and kissed her on the cheek, then turned on the news. The boys ran to greet their dad, and the noise level in the house rose. The teasing, picking, and harassing began between Brad and his two boys. Jackie asked them to keep it down because the girls were still studying, but the chaos continued. The noise was almost more than she could tolerate.

Then she heard little Sara crying. Jackie asked Brad to stir the meat and ran upstairs to check on Sara. She had slammed her finger in the cabinet. Jackie held her in her arms and carried her downstairs. She smelled something burning and noticed that Drew was in his recliner. Smoke rose from the pot, as did her anger with her husband, whom she had left in charge of the cooking meat.

With Sara on her hip, thoughts of self-pity consumed her mind. They don't care about what you ask them to do. They don't appreciate anything you do. You will become some old woman no one likes. Your husband is not interested in you. You are fat and ugly and will one day be all alone. The romance you long for is never going to happen. Your husband is more interested in the six o'clock news and aggravating the kids than in you. Your family is dysfunctional, loud, and annoying and will never change. No other family acts like this. They all get along and show love and consideration. Your children and husband act like that because of you. You don't pray enough. They don't see Christ in you. You are not a good mother or wife.

Today's homework will look a little different from most Day 5 lessons. Look back at each day's lesson for this week, and copy the lie we studied on the corresponding line below. On the second line, identify whether Jackie had taken the bait and explain why you believe she did or did not.

Lie #1—_____
Did Jackie take the bait? Explain. _____
_____

Lie #2—_____
Did Jackie take the bait? Explain. _____
_____

Lie #3—_____
Did Jackie take the bait? Explain. _____
_____

Lie #4—_____
Did Jackie take the bait? Explain. _____
_____

If you were going to give Jackie wise, godly counsel and encouragement, what passages of Scripture that we studied this week would you use, and why? (Feel free to add other verses too.)

_____

_____

_____

_____

During this week of study, were you able to identify any lies you might be believing at this very moment? If so, ask God to show you a passage of Scripture that specifically trumps that lie, and write it down.

_____

_____

_____

# WEEK 6

## GOD'S ARMOR FOR WOMEN—PART 1

For the next two weeks, we will spend our time in the last chapter of Ephesians, looking at the apostle Paul's teaching about spiritual battle. Our goal is to take one topic at a time and investigate its meaning and impact in our lives. I am so proud of you for sticking to this and doing the hard work of equipping yourself with the necessary knowledge and understanding to be empowered to live victoriously. You are doing great. Hang in there—just two more weeks, and you will be equipped and empowered women of God!

### Day 1
### Stand Firm with Truth

This week our study focuses on one passage of Scripture relating to the weapons of our warfare, Ephesians 6:10–18. Today our attention centers on the weapon of truth. Truth is the opposite of a lie; its antonym is dishonesty.

Read Ephesians 6:10–16.

In verse 14, we are instructed: "_____ firm then, with the belt of _____ buckled around your waist."

Truth is where our strategy begins. If not built on truth, our armor will be a foundation of sinking sand. The weapons of our warfare are not mighty unless we know truth and believe truth to be truth. We began this study series with the question Pontius Pilate posed to Jesus: "What is truth?" We learned the truth that God has a good plan for our lives and the enemy has a plan to steal, to kill, and to destroy. However, there is more to truth than a what; there's also a who. Jesus said, "I am the way and the truth and the life" (John 14:6). He also declared, "I came to bring truth to the world. All who love the truth recognize that what I say is true" (John 18:37).

Look back at Week 3, Day 1, and read the fill-in-the-blank section from John 1:1–3 and 14.

> The word of the Lord is right and all His work is done in truth.
>
> Psalm 33:4

Jesus is the Word of God, full of grace and truth. He came to be truth, to bring truth, to say truth, and to do truth. In Titus 1:2, Paul stated, "God can not lie."

Read Luke 20:20–26. What does verse 21 say Jesus did not do?

_____

How did those attempting to trap Jesus in His words react to His answer?

_____

The Pharisees, the ones who thought they had it all together, wanted to seal Jesus' lips once and for all. They sent spies, hoping to trap Him, because they did not understand the absence of lies and deceit in Jesus. They had seen a man speaking in a way that showed no personal favoritism toward anyone. I wonder if that was the Pharisees' biggest reason for hating Him.

When someone has an ego problem, that person wants everyone to know how great he or she is. But the words that came from Jesus did not acknowledge them to be any more special than the beggar, the lame, the unclean, the sinner, the gentile, etc. Jesus was an equal-opportunity guy.

Do you know someone who tries to make you feel less valuable than he or she is? If so, explain how that person does this.

_____

I will praise You, for I am fearfully and wonderfully made;marvelous
are You works and that my soul knows very well.
Psalm 139:14 (NKJV)

After reading the truth in Psalm 139:14, how might you respond when someone tries to devalue who you are?

_____

Truth shows no partiality. Truth is truth. Everyone faces truth on a level playing field. I remember when my church prepared for an Easter program. The program was one of song, with interpretive movements done by people of all ages, races, shapes, and sizes. The people in the program were asked to dress as they would on any normal day, whether in holey jeans or a business suit, because the message being sent was that we all come to the cross of Jesus exactly the same way. Truth is unchanging, no matter who you are, because truth is not based on who we are but on who He is. "Jesus Christ is the same yesterday, today, and forever" (Hebrews 13:8 NKJV).

As the world around us wavers, isn't it time for some consistency in our lives? My most heartfelt encouragement to you is to get your eyes off of people and look to Jesus. Even Christians will fail you. Don't let the mistakes of a human be your only testimony of our Lord. Stand firm, and buckle up with Jesus Christ. Put on your first layer of armor by wrapping your waist with truth.

# Day 2
# Stand Firm with Righteousness

Dear sister, you will notice that your instructions today mirror yesterday's opening. Please don't skim through the reading because you just did it yesterday. God's word is living. What you hear today may be different than what He revealed to you yesterday. Also, realize that repetition is one basic method of learning, the kind of learning that gets down into the core of your being. That kind of learning will equip and empower you for the spiritual battle.

Read Ephesians 6:10–16, and fill in the blanks from verse 14.
"_____ firm then, with the belt of _____ buckled around your waist, with the breastplate of _____ in place."

Looking at the original Greek language, the breastplate of righteousness as pictured here involves not only wearing but sinking into a garment. I have an oversized faux fur coat that is so long, it reaches my ankles. When I put it on, I feel submerged in depths of comfort and protection from the cold. The breastplate of righteousness is bigger than we are, and immersing ourselves in it brings us to a place of comfort and protection from the enemy.

I don't know about you, but righteousness is not a trait I feel well endowed with most of the time. If fighting the good fight requires a breastplate of righteousness, how am I going to wear a breastplate of righteousness when I am all-too-well acquainted with the my own lack of righteousness?

All of us have become like one who is unclean, and all our righteous acts are like filthy rags; we all shrivel up like a leaf, and like the wind our sins sweep us away.
Isaiah 64:6 (NIV)

Let Isaiah 64:6 remind you of yesterday's lesson, where we learned that Jesus does not show partiality for any reason. Being better than the next person is simply not good enough, because the best we can be will never measure up to God's standard. "All have sinned and fall short of the glory of God" (Romans 3:23 NKJV). If we are all unclean, and we all fall short, how will we ever put on the breastplate of righteousness?

Read the following passages, and write on the line above each verse what that verse says about righteousness.

_____

Blessed are those who hunger and thirst for righteousness, for they shall be filled.
Matthew 5:6

_____

Seek first the kingdom of God and His righteousness,
and all these things shall be added to you.
Matthew 6:33

_____

For in it the righteousness of God is revealed from faith to
faith; as it is written, "The just shall live by faith."
Romans 1:17

_____

To him who does not work but believes on Him who justifies
the ungodly, his faith is accounted for righteousness.
Romans 4:5

_____

With the heart one believes unto righteousness, and with
the mouth confession is made unto salvation.
Romans 10:10

He made Him who knew no sin to be sin for us, that we
might become the righteousness of God in Him.
2 Corinthians 5:21

And be found in Him, not having my own righteousness, which is from the law, but that which is through faith in Christ, the righteousness which is from God by faith.
Philippians 3:9 (NKJV)

How much of righteousness is dependent on how good you are? _____
What is your role in having righteousness?

_____

Take what you have learned throughout this study of righteousness, and explain how you will sink into your breastplate of righteousness.

_____

_____

# Day 3
# Stand Firm with Readiness

Do you have a fresh understanding or view of truth and righteousness after our past two days of study together? I hope so. Your reading for today is still the same. Please, please, don't get so familiar that you browse through the words rather than relish the words of Scripture!

Read Ephesians 6:10–16, and fill in the blanks from verses 14 and 15.

"_____ firm then, with the belt of _____ buckled around your waist, with the breastplate of _____ in place, and with your feet fitted with the _____ that comes from the gospel of _____."

There are times when, as students of God's Word, reading and rereading familiar Scriptures, we may think there is nothing new we can learn. The funny thing about God is, just when you think you have learned all you can learn, He shows you a different angle you never saw before. His Spirit brings to attention the things He wants us to see when He wants us to see them.

The Lord gave me a fresh insight on Ephesians 6:15. Usually, when I think about this part of the armor, I think of wearing the shoes of the gospel of peace. Today, the word *readiness* hit me like a baseball bat. We are told to wear the readiness of the gospel (the Greek meaning for *gospel* is "good news").

The original Greek word translated *readiness* in verse 15 means preparing and being prepared. Ephesians 6:15 is the one time in the New Testament that this word is linked to military use. The *Complete Word Study Dictionary of the New Testament* states, "This intimates the firm and solid knowledge of the gospel in which the believer may stand firm and unmoved like soldiers in military duty." The original meaning emphasizes being prepared with the knowledge of the gospel. Therefore, our success in the battle hinges largely on our preparedness and knowledge of the gospel of peace.

Let's spend the rest of this lesson focusing on the gospel of peace. Did you wonder why Paul didn't say the gospel of Jesus Christ? Ephesians 2:14 identifies Jesus as our peace. Why peace? On Week 3, Day 3, we learned to hold on to our peace knowing that the Lord fights for us. Jesus gives peace, and His peace is unlike the world's peace (John 14:27).

> I have told you these things, so that in me you may have peace. In this world
> you will have trouble. But take heart! I have overcome the world.
> John 16:33 (NIV)

In what way might His peace be different from the world's peace?

_____

Read Proverbs 16:7. What does God do when He is pleased with us?

_____

Read Philippians 4:7. What does the peace of God do?

_____

Have you ever experienced God's peace guarding your heart and mind at a time when peace made no sense at all? If so, explain.

_____

_____

Death is a harsh reality and can be one of the most devastating experiences when we lose someone we love. However, I have seen a distinction between those who know Christ and those who do not. There is always a peace about the believer that, in natural terms, does not add up. The peace should not be there, but it is, because Christ makes a difference. Isaiah 26:3 tells us how to experience perfect peace in our daily lives.

Read Isaiah 26:3, and write down how we can be kept in perfect peace.

_____

# Day 4
# In Addition to All This

Paul's teaching has equipped us with the knowledge of truth and righteousness and emphasized the necessity of being ready with the good news of Jesus Christ. Today's lesson has a mathematical connotation, beginning with a necessary add-on. The three other lessons are crucial, but this one, the other three can't do without.

Blueberry pie without blueberries isn't blueberry pie. A coat in a closet has no value if you're outside in twenty-degree weather, and the past three days of standing firm won't accomplish much if we don't take up the shield of faith.

Please reread Ephesians 6:10–16, zeroing in on verse 16, and fill in the blanks below.

"In addition to all this, _____ up the _____ of _____."

According to Ephesians 6:16, what is the value of taking up the shield of faith?

_____

Our enemy uses us as target practice, seeing if his arrows can penetrate our belief system. Where are we strong in our faith? That is where we are holding up the shield, and his evil shots can't get through. In what areas do we struggle with believing God? Those are the devil's delight, the places he can penetrate and sometimes defeat us because we don't believe. He is at work because he knows if he can find and attack us in a spot of unbelief, there is his greatest potential to rule over us.

Look at the end of Day 4's lesson from last week. Explain how 1 John 5:4 and Ephesians 6:16 are equal.

_____

_____

Hebrews 11:1 (NKJV) defines faith as "the substance of things hoped for, the evidence of things not seen." Substance means material or tangible physical matter. Are you scratching your head wondering how tangible matter and the unseen go together? Faith is the tangible physical matter of things hoped for, and faith is the evidence or proof of things unseen. Believing does not mean seeing, but believing can be seen. Faith in a life is observable.

In Mark 2, a paralytic is brought to Jesus to be healed. The four men who brought the man could not get to the door because of the crowds. They took the paralytic on top of the house and lowered him through the roof to Jesus. The Bible records that Jesus saw their faith. Faith is seen because it compels us to do things we otherwise would never have done. There is action to faith: sometimes it's a pursuit, sometimes it is waiting, and sometimes it's a change in direction.

> Faith by itself, if it is not accompanied by action, is dead.
> James 2:17 (NIV)

List some ways you have seen faith in action.

_____

_____

Abraham went. Noah built. Hebrews 11 is packed with stories of men and women acting out what they believed in their hearts. Our beliefs affect what we do.

Describe tangible ways your faith affects you and others.

_____

_____

_____

# Day 5
# Day of Fiction—Apply God's Word

Our story today tells of a woman damaged by Satan's lies but who seeks to overcome the lies and replace them with truth. If she continues on that path, she will be victorious! You can be victorious too. As you read the story, identify Satan's lies. If there is a lie or lies you identify with, make a notation of it in the margin.

Valerie rose early, fixed a cup of coffee, gathered her books, and headed to the back porch swing. She read God's Word and prayed while her family was nestled in their beds. She whispered, "Lord, show me what You say about me. What is the truest thing about me, Lord?" She turned the page of her Bible, and her eyes fell upon these words: "The LORD will hold you in His hands for all to see—a splendid crown in the hands of God" (Isaiah 62:3, NLT). Her heart was awakened, and she was in awe. She whispered again, "Me, Lord? Really, really?" She heard His gentle whisper to her heart, "Yes, you, Valerie. I have chosen you, and you are my beloved!"

Flashbacks from her horrific divorce seven years earlier punctured her moment of bliss. She heard, "Now, really, you—splendid? What if people saw you then? Splendid and beloved would not be the words they would use to describe you. More like tramp. Failure. Not good enough." The thoughts pierced her still frail heart. She didn't want anyone to see those days, nor did she want to relive them. The mess she had made. The heartache she'd endured. Through the whole, ugly season, she had accepted the failures and mistakes as part of who she was. How could it be possible that she would be seen as splendid before her Creator or anyone else? She longed to be splendid, noticed, delighted in, seen as beautiful, invited, and valued. But she felt more like a mess, a failure, with too much baggage, too needy, and definitely not good enough to captivate another's heart.

Drawn back to God's Word, she read, "O storm battered city, troubled and desolate. I will rebuild you on a foundation of sapphires and make the walls of your houses like precious jewels. I will make your towers of sparkling rubies and your gates and walls of shining gems" (Isaiah 54:11–12). She pulled His truth close to her heart and relished the fact that the God of the beginning and the end, who sees everything, who is all-knowing and all-powerful, was romancing her and drawing her to himself.

Valerie sipped her coffee and glided back and forth on the swing. The wind caressed her golden hair, and she sensed a peace and love for her Savior like never before. She verbalized her praise to God, and the lies of her past faded. She heard His words: "I have come to heal the brokenhearted and set the captives free; to bestow on them a crown of beauty instead of ashes. The King is enthralled with your beauty. My eyes search the whole earth to strengthen those whose eyes are fixed on Me. I am my beloved's and He is mine." She was mesmerized by the truth of His love for her. She had been taught it her entire life but never really experienced Him in this way—ever. For the first time in her thirty-seven years, she was smitten with her Savior. Nothing had ever filled the emptiness in her heart until now. No job, no man, no child, no perfect vacation, not even a fine pair of boots.

Jesus swept her off her feet and filled her soul. She continued to swing back and forth, and she remembered the words she had read from a devotional a few days earlier: "the root of holiness is romance." She smiled sweetly, closed her eyes, and breathed deeply. "Yes. Lord, I am a woman who is battered, broken, and unclean. Nothing about me is holy. But in Your unfailing love, You are calling me out and drawing me to Yourself. And there, in Your presence, and rooted in Your love, You romance me and cover me with Your truth, the truth of who I really am. Your holiness alone transforms my stains and redeems my heart. Thank You, my Beloved."

Explain how you see Valerie putting on the belt of truth. (Day 1)

_____


Have you ever had a mental battle similar to Valerie's while in the midst of time with God, when the enemy taunted you with his lies? Identify the lies, and explain your struggle.

_____

_____


I love the way this story portrays God countering the enemy's lies, speaking His truth to Valerie. She was seeking, and God was speaking! Throughout this week, we have identified truth that overrules the lies of the enemy. What Bible verse from this week's study would you tell Valerie to mediate on if you knew her? Why?

_____

_____

_____

Look back at the story and underline how Valerie saw her own righteousness. At what point does Valerie pick up the breastplate of righteousness and put it on? (Day 2)

_____

_____

Valerie seemed to assume a posture of peace. On what basis does it appear that she was able to do that? (Day 3)

_____

Give examples of how Valerie had tangible faith. (Day 4)

_____

_____

# WEEK 7

## GOD'S ARMOR FOR WOMEN—PART 2

Congratulations! You are rounding the final bend in our study and are headed for the finish line. I hope you have learned and grown in your relationship with God and your understanding of the spiritual battle. Last week we learned that hope is a confident expectation, and that is the kind of hope I have for you. I can have that kind of hope based on the truth of God's Word, which He promises will do what He intended it to do (Isaiah 55:11). It will go forth and won't return to God void, and you and I have been all up in the Word of God. His Word is working in and on both me and you!

I love working out and knowing the end is in just a few more minutes or a few more exercises. At that point, I find the strength to dig down deep within myself and increase the intensity a notch or two more. Dear sister, dig down deep and increase your focus. Finish strong!

## Day 1
## Helmet of Salvation

I know you are thinking, Oh my goodness! You are kidding me! We have to read this same passage of Scripture again this week? Well, fortunately, yes. This week, the passage should be really familiar to you—so much so that you should be on the brink of memorizing it and without even realizing it.

I want us to make that a reality by the end of this week. Yes, I want you and I to commit to memorizing Ephesians 6:10–16. Memorization is not nearly as hard as we make it out to be, and the value of memorizing Scripture far exceeds the struggle to get it etched into our minds. My favorite method of memorization is writing the verses on index cards and carrying them with me wherever I go. That way you can read them throughout the day, at red lights in traffic, in the pick-up line at your child's school, on a break at work… Consider every free moment an opportunity to hide God's Word in your heart.

Read Ephesians 6:10–17

> Take the helmet of salvation and the sword of the Spirit,
> which is the word of God. Ephesians 6:17 (NIV)

A helmet is usually a hard, protective covering worn on the head, where the brain is located. Helmets are designed to protect the head from injury. Helmets from the period when Paul wrote his letter were normally made of bronze. There is no doubt why the helmet of salvation is a necessary part of our armor. The mind must be protected, because it is the devil's playground. We have seen throughout this Bible study many ways the enemy attacks our minds.

However, this is not just any helmet—it's the helmet of salvation. Why would Paul find it necessary to distinguish it as the helmet of salvation? Why not the helmet of courage? Why not the helmet of joy, peace, or something else we need to have protecting our minds? Paul knew the damage the enemy could do to the kingdom of God if he could make a believer in Christ doubt his or her salvation.

> But since we belong to the day, let us be self-controlled, putting on faith
> and love as a breastplate, and the hope of salvation as a helmet.
> 1 Thessalonians 5:8

Circle what Paul added to the helmet of salvation in 1 Thessalonians 5:8 (above).

The hope referred to in the Bible is not like what we think of as hope today. Most of us think hope is similar to wishing. In fact, many of us might say the two words could be used interchangeably. I looked up the synonyms for hope on my computer, and *wish* was one of them.

However, looking at the meaning of *hope* in the understanding of the early Christians and even in pre-Christianity, it is a long way from wishing. Wishing on a star may make a cute childhood song, but it won't carry us very far in life. Hope as used in 1 Thessalonians 5:8, according to the *Complete Word Study Dictionary of the New Testament*, means "desire of something good with expectation of obtaining it." My online study tools put it like this: "joyful and confident expectation of eternal salvation." The difference is, wishing is wishing; hope is expecting!

For the first few years of my salvation, I could not put on the helmet of salvation because I was not sure. I constantly battled thoughts like, There is no way you are saved. If you were, you would not still... You've done too much in your past—God could not possibly forgive all that. I prayed the sinner's prayer every time someone led it in a church service because I wasn't sure if it had worked the time before.

Does any of this sound familiar? I am not sure at what point everything changed for me. I do not have a memory of a particular event, but I know how the realization came that I was truly saved.

I kept pursuing God. I went to church. I read my Bible. I could not let go. I so desperately wanted salvation that I continued to hang on to any glimmer of hope. This kept me close to Jesus. I understand the heart of David when he said, "But now, Lord, what do I look for? My hope is in you" (Psalm 39:7, NIV). Jesus did not let me down. He was faithful to show me my salvation, enabling me to put on my helmet every day. Now, this is easy for me.

Now I understand that salvation is not found in any thing I do or don't do, outside of believing. Salvation is in Christ alone. Not knowing and believing in our own salvation is like having a handicap. On the other hand, knowing and believing in our salvation empowers us to live above our natural capabilities and keep the enemy under our feet!

Is there an area where you feel the enemy has been having a heyday harassing you, keeping you beaten down, discouraging you, tempting you, etc.? If so, what is it?

_____

Read Ephesians 3:19–23.

Do you believe the kind of power in this verse is enough to put the enemy in his place and win the battle you identified in the space above?

_____

After all you've studied today, why would the helmet of salvation be necessary to experience the power of Christ in defeating the enemy in your life?

_____

_____

## Day 2
## Sword of the Spirit

I hope you are taking the memorization exercise seriously and with a positive attitude. Attitude does really matter. If you say, "I can't do that," guess what? You probably won't. But if you have the attitude, "I can do all things through Christ who strengthens me" (Philippians 4:13), and if you believe that the Holy Spirit will bring God's Word to your memory (John 14:26), you probably will memorize Ephesians 6:10-17 by the end of the week.

Read Ephesians 6:10–17

> Take the helmet of salvation and the sword of the Spirit,
> which is the word of God. Ephesians 6:17 (NIV)

The Sword of the spirit is an offensive weapon. There is no other offensive weapon listed in the whole armor of God in Ephesians 6:10–17. You don't have to look far to know what the Spirit's sword is. Fill in the blanks below according to Ephesians 6:17.

The sword of the Spirit is the _____ of _____.

The commentary on Ephesians 6:17 in my *Nelson's New King James Study Bible* says: "The weapon is not necessarily the Bible as a whole, but the specific word that needs to be spoken in a specific situation. To have the precise word ready, a person must know the Bible intimately."

Read Matthew 4:3–4. What did Jesus declare that we live on?

_____

Jesus knew God's Word. Satan tempted Jesus with an explicit temptation. Jesus responded with a specific word at the exact moment needed. In Matthew 4:4, Jesus declared that people live not by bread alone but on every word from the mouth of God. We were created to live on and by God's Word. A specific word from God at your most desperate moments breathes fresh life into you and your circumstances. When the Most High God speaks, there is no greater delight and no greater power!

While rocking on my front porch one morning and reading my Bible, I saw a fat, ugly spider (I hate spiders). I stopped and searched for a weapon in the garage. Armed with a green can of wasp and hornet spray, I marched back to the spider, aimed, and fired. I do not know whether it died from poison or drowning, but it's dead. Once back in my chair, I thought about the reasons I had felt compelled to kill the spider. I'd seen the spider as a potential danger. If left there, the spider would have had opportunity to bite me or someone I love and would reproduce, creating more threatening spiders.

What if Jesus had not spoken to the enemy? What if He had left him unchecked to continue to speak poisonous lies and present dangerous temptations? As Christians, we overlook the power of God's Word to help us, empower us, and deliver us from dangerous situations. When we overlook the power of God's Word in our circumstances, we allow the enemy to build webs of deceit in our lives. Ladies, we have been given a weapon like no other, but we must know and use the weapon.

Read Hebrews 4:12.

How is the Word of God described?

_____

What does the Word of God do?

_____

Look back at the beginning of today's lesson, and read Ephesians 6:17 again.

The original Greek word for *sword* in Ephesians 6:17 speaks of a large knife used for killing animals and cutting up flesh. The word originated from the context of one-on-one combat.

Over the past few years, I have attended various writers' conferences. One overemphasized point is that writing should be clear and concise. One way to clean up writing is to take out prepositions and use fewer words to convey the same or the most precise meaning. In "the sword of the Spirit," "of the Spirit" is a prepositional phrase. How can you write a phrase with the same meaning but with fewer words? I will give you a hint and an example. Hint: Think possessive. Example: Tom's cat.

Write your revision: _____

Finish today's lesson by asking the Holy Spirit to help you see His sword as He sees it. Sketch a picture of a sword in the space below, and write words around the sword that identify, describe, and distinguish the sword of the Spirit from just any old sword. (Art lessons aren't required. Just give it your best shot.)

# Day 3
# Pray

Is your head covered with the helmet of salvation? Do you have the Holy Spirit's sword in your hand? I hope so! How are you doing with memorizing Ephesians 6:10–16? Don't give up! You can do it! We are close to the finish line, but these last three days may be the most important lessons of the study. You know what to do. Read Ephesians 6:10–17.

> Pray in the Spirit on all occasions with all kinds of prayers and requests. With this in mind, be alert and always keep on praying for all the Lord's people.
> Ephesians 6:18 (NIV)

A clear picture is painted looking at what various Bible translations say about when we should pray—not just on my knees or in my bed, not only in the morning, but every waking moment. NIV uses the words "on all occasions." NKJV uses "always," ASV "at all seasons," and HCSB "at all times." NLT gets redundant, saying we should pray "at all times and on every occasion." Do you get the message?

Read Jesus' parable in Luke 18:1–8.

In your own words, explain the meaning of the parable.

_____

Praying is not part of the armor, but it is an essential element in winning the spiritual battle. James 4:2 tells us that we do not have because we do not ask. Persistence and perseverance in our prayers are key factors in getting an answer from God, as we see in Luke 18:1–5. There are seasons when God seals His holy lips shut, and we have to pursue Him with everything in us to get a word from Him. James 4:3 explains that a prayer life focused on selfish pleasure will lead to unanswered prayers as well. How can we pray and be assured of a heavenly answer?

Read 1 John 5:14–15.

When can we be confident that God will hear our prayers?

_____

What can we be confident about if we know that God hears our prayers?

_____

Ephesians 6:18 (above) says that we are to always pray in the _____.

Look back over Day 2's lesson. The Word of God is also known as the sword of the _____ or, in my preferred wording, the Holy Spirit's _____.

Find the cause and effect in each of the verses below.

Romans 10:17
Cause _____
Effect _____

2 Corinthians 4:13
Cause _____
Effect _____

John 15:7
Cause _____
Effect _____

It is important that we bring two things together. The heart of Jesus' words in John 15:7 may give us the greatest insight as to how praying in the Spirit and the sword of the Spirit interact, releasing a holy "Yes." Link the two phrases by making a sentence using the word from the box that you think best completes the sentence below.

| Using | believing | wielding | exerting | exercising | speaking |
|-------|-----------|----------|----------|------------|----------|

Pray in the Spirit, _____ the sword of the Spirit. Amen!

# Day 4
# Keep On Praying

What a way to round that final bend of this seven-week journey of getting armed for spiritual battle, with "Keep on Praying." The battles we face will be best won on our knees, our faces, or even our bottoms, conversing with God. Let's wrap up by revisiting the lessons learned yesterday. Retention is greater when we study and restudy.

We learned that God answers our prayers with a yes when we ask according to His will. We discovered that His Word affects our answers to our prayers and that hearing His Word brings faith; therefore, we speak what we believe. In case you are wondering which word was the correct one to fill in the blank above, the answer is all or any of them.

What was the main lesson about prayer, from Luke 18:1–8, on Day 3?

_____

Read Luke 11:5–13.

What appears to be the main point or message Jesus is communicating in these verses?

_____

Is there something that you have needed from God for a long time? _____

If you answered yes, take a moment to answer the questions below.

1.  Have you specifically asked God for this? _____
2.  Write the reason your request is with or without a wrong motive?

    _____

3.  Can you say your prayer lines up with God's will?

    _____

4.  What passage of Scripture gives evidence of the unity of your prayer and God's will? _____
5.  How long have you prayed for this? _____
6.  How long are you willing to pray for this? _____

Let's take a turn toward the Old Testament. Let me set up the story before you begin. Ahab, king of Israel, "did evil in the sight of the Lord, more than all who were before him" (1 Kings 16:30). Ahab worshipped Baal and believed that Baal controlled the dew and rain. Elijah, a prophet, declared in the face of Ahab and in the name of the Lord God of Israel that there would be no rain in the land except by his word (1 Kings 17:1). There was no rain for three years.

Read 1 Kings 18:41–45, and identify what actions by Elijah brought rain.

_____

_____

This message has personal meaning for me, and I hope it hits home for you too. I have prayed for four years for one particular thing to happen and seen little result. However, I see a cloud the size of a man's hand. I believe the answers to my prayers are just around the corner, and I am praying until the answer comes. Rain is coming!

I am so proud of you! I love you and have delighted in writing this material. It is my greatest desire to see your relationship with Jesus grow and your knowledge of truth empower you to defeat the enemy. Press on. Stand firm. See the salvation of the Lord. Amen.

# Day 5
# Day of Nonfiction—Apply God's Word

You made it! I know I've said it already, but I am super proud of you for choosing to work through this to the end. I pray that you are better equipped and empowered to face the unseen battle that is a part of everyday real life. This final day of study has a different twist: it is an overview of my story before I knew Jesus. The preschool and elementary school parts of the story are only vague generalizations from distant memories, but beginning with my teenage years, the memories and the story are very specific.

Over the past six weeks, I have given you directions on Day 5 pertaining to the points addressed in the Bible study for that week. Today I would like for you to read the story and think through all you have learned over the past few weeks. Identify the enemy at work and the Lord at work and any understanding of truth that could be applied to this life and circumstances. Use your Bible study as a resource guide to help you.

### Pat Domangue's True Story

**Preschool**
"Why can't you pay attention? Can't you do anything right?" The shamed little girl stared at the puddle of red Kool-Aid on her mother's brand-new carpet. She did not notice the weight of that chain.

**Third Grade**
"You must be dumb," the teacher told her in front of the whole class when she could not get her math right. She barely noticed the weight of that chain.

**Teenager**
The young man's lack of interest assured her that her thoughts were true: She thought: He must think I'm ugly. I'm not good enough. My nose is too big. My teeth aren't perfect. I wish I had blonde hair, not brown. He's right, I am ugly. Another chain.

The shame, guilt, and blame of a sexual assault proved to be more than she could take. She was sure there was only one way out, so two weeks after enduring the assault, she emptied two bottles of pills into her tiny frame. In the darkness of that night, she cried out to the God she had heard about in church. "If You will save me, I won't ever do this again." He heard. But she still felt the heavy weight of many chains.

She had to pick herself up and go on, because no one could help her. She could not go back in time, so she learned to put on a hard outer shell. More chains.

At sixteen, the pregnancy test was positive. Chains. She got married, had a miscarriage, and got a divorce in less than a year. Chains. She wondered what Jesus thought of her now. She never thought her life could be so messed up. But there was no way out—or was there?

**Adult**

A job, a new car, and looking good—look out world, here she comes. Nightclubs, partying, and outward happiness, but an inner emptiness ruled her heart. How could it be fixed? She remembered Jesus. No, she could not go that way—she was too messed up. More chains.

She met the man of her dreams in a bar. Surely he would fill the void in her heart. He was great. He had a great job and spent all his money on taking her out and partying. One year and two months later, she married him. The void remained. More chains.

Introduced to New Age and the idea of reincarnation, she began to read one occult book after another. Something triggered her thoughts, hearkening back to all those years growing up in church. Occult? Wasn't that something bad? Nah. Besides, the people in church were not all they were cracked up to be anyway. They had not seemed very Christian-like when the church split. There was all that arguing and gossip. No, this way seemed better. She could do what she wanted as long she didn't hurt anyone. And what is true for one may not necessarily be true for another. Heavy chains.

The person she held most dear died from a sudden heart attack. Why would God take her daddy? What would she do? She knew she must go on because of her precious little two-year-old girl. Two years later, a second little girl was born into this very dysfunctional life. Chains.

She tried church again, but when opposition came, she went back to the occult books, each a little deeper and darker than the one before. Chains.

Divorce number two and man number three. Chains.

He must be the one who will change it all. She and man number three got married, but she thought they should go to church because her children needed to be raised in church.

Tired and weighted down, she wondered why she couldn't find peace and fulfillment. This man was really great, but she was still hurting. She remembered Jesus. She heard Him calling. She responded to His call, and Jesus began to remove a lifetime of chains, one at a time.

It's your turn to identify the enemy at work and the Lord at work in this story, as well as any understanding of truth that can be applied to this girl's life and circumstances. Use your Bible study as a resource guide to help you.

_____

_____

_____

_____

_____

_____

_____

_____

_____

_____

_____

_____

_____

Well, dear sister in Christ, you did it!

I am so proud of you and thankful that you did the hard word it took to complete this study. You are in a spiritual battle, but you have learned the basic premise of that battle and the character and strategies of your enemy. You know you can trust God as your provider and rely on His strength, knowing that He is in control and that He loves you and will never leave you.

You should also now know more about your personal weaknesses and your strength in Christ. You can see more clearly Satan's deceptive ways and lies, and you know the significance of the spiritual armor we have to defend against his evil work.

You are now equipped and empowered to live a victorious life in Christ!

Until we study together again,

Stay strong in the Lord and in His mighty power.
Ephesians 6:10